O N E H O U R W I Z

OneHourWiz™

Stock Options

By

Vivian A. Wagner, Ph.D.

ASPATORE
BOOKS

Published by Aspatore Books, Inc.
For information on bulk orders, sponsorship opportunities, licensing, author speaking engagements or any other questions please email store@aspatore.com. For corrections, comments or any other inquiries please email info@aspatore.com.

First Printing,
10 9 8 7 6 5 4 3 2 1

ISBN: 1-58762-105-3

Cover design by James Weinberg, Kara Yates

Special thanks to Ben Lewis and Melissa Conradi for their excellent editing!

This book is printed on acid free paper.

OneHourWiz™

The Legendary, World-Famous Method to Mastering Anything in an Hour

How do I become a OneHourWiz?

OneHourWiz is a proven, unique method of learning that focuses on the fundamental principles of a topic, along with advice from industry experts, to master the most important aspects of anything in an hour. Although not always known by the name OneHourWiz, the principles behind this important method of learning have been practiced for decades by leading executives of the world's largest companies, top government officials, federal intelligence agencies, and some of the world's most renowned professors, teachers and visionaries.

Most people do not realize that when trying to learn a new subject or topic, they spend 80% of their time not focusing on the right principles. If they were to receive instruction from the right teachers, focused on the right principles, they could learn anything in a fraction of the time. However, getting all of these industry leaders, teachers and visionaries together would be virtually impossible. Therefore, our OneHourWiz authors collect the most important pieces of information from these individuals, pour through volumes of research, talk with industry leaders and present the material in a condensed and easy to understand format.

So, how is it possible to master anything in an hour? Each OneHourWiz uses a proprietary method that focuses on 8 core areas including: The 10 Most Important Principles, The History/Background Information, Focal Points, Interviews With Industry Visionaries, Excerpts From Experienced Individuals (Quick Tips), Case Studies & Worksheets, Resources for Further Research, and a Key Words Glossary so you can "talk the talk." OneHourWiz guides have become overnight classics that remain with our readers for years and years as timeless guides they can always refer back to. So sit back, relax, and enjoy the following pages on your way to becoming a OneHourWiz!

About Aspatore Books
www.Aspatore.com

Aspatore Books has become one of the leading book publishing houses in record setting time by combining the best aspects of traditional book publishing with the new abilities enabled by the Internet and technology. Aspatore Books publishes the Inside the Minds, Bigwig Briefs, OneHourWiz and Aspatore Business Review imprints in addition to other best selling non-fiction and fiction books. Aspatore Books is focused on infusing creativity, innovation and interaction into the book publishing industry and providing a heightened experience for readers worldwide. Aspatore Books focuses on publishing traditional print books, while our two portfolio companies, Big Brand Books and Publishville.com focus on developing areas within the book publishing world. Aspatore Books is committed to providing our readers, authors, bookstores, distributors and customers with the highest quality books, book related services, and publishing execution available anywhere in the world.

Become a Part of
OneHourWiz™

- Publish a Quick Tip on an Upcoming Topic (50-5,000 words)
- Submit an Idea to Write an Entire OneHourWiz
- Post Comments on the Topics Mentioned
- Read Expanded Excerpts
- Free Excerpts From Upcoming Guides
- Links for More Information on a Topic

www.OneHourWiz.com

Order These Other Great OneHourWiz™ Guides Today!

OneHourWiz: Making Your First Million
By Jon Pirone, ISBN: 1587621037
OneHourWiz: Making Your First Million presents ways for every individual to make their first million. Three main focal areas are covered including investing, starting your own business, and taking equity as a form of compensation. The guide is a very practical and entertaining look at ways for anyone to make their first million. The guide also includes interviews with some of the most successful business people of our time who explain how they "made their first million."

OneHourWiz: Becoming a Techie
By Mary Pyefinch, ISBN: 1587621045
OneHourWiz: Becoming a Techie is a whirlwind tour of computer technology presented in an easy to understand language and format that both technology novices and experts will find useful and entertaining. Readers will learn about computers, networks, programming, the Internet, telecommunications and wireless. After reading this guide, any individual will have the knowledge and guidance to "talk the talk" of the techies. The guide also includes interviews with leading CTOs from companies such as Motley Fool, Symantec, Verisign, Flooz.com and others who help break down the language of the techies!

OneHourWiz: Personal PR & Making a Name For Yourself
By Colleen Inches, ISBN: 1587621061
Have you ever wished you could sell yourself the way advertisers promote products? Wouldn't you love to say, "Hey world, here I am. I'm the best product in the market!" It's no coincidence the most successful people in business do it everyday, and so can you. Colleen Burns Inches shows you how to use self promotion in any career or aspect of your life. Inches, a former television news producer in New York City, gives you step by step instructions on getting attention, recognition and even media coverage for your ideas and events.

OneHourWiz: Internet Freelancing (Easy to Implement Ways to Making a Little or a Lot of Extra Money on the Internet)
By Rachel Vine, ISBN: 1587620030
OneHourWiz: Internet Freelancing contains the most up to date information on how to use the Internet to make a little, or a lot, of extra money on the Internet. The guide covers every opportunity available on the Internet including getting Paid-to-Surf the web, test new Internet products and services, freelance writing, part time consulting opportunities, affiliate programs, or simply getting paid on a monthly basis by having an extra task bar on your browser. Whether you are looking to make an extra $25 a month or an extra $2,500 a month, this guide will pay for itself many times over within the first month alone.

OneHourWiz: Internet and Technology Careers (After the Shakedown)
By April Griffin, ISBN: 1587620049
Want to take advantage of the perks Internet and technology companies have to offer? This guide will help make sure you know what to look for, ask the right questions, and get the right things put into writing so you have your upside (such as options and bonuses) and downside (guaranteed employment clauses) covered. You've heard the hype. Now learn how to use all the buzzwords with authority. Discover the workplace trends - where the hot jobs can be found, the training you need, and the salary to expect. Read interviews with recruiters from international job placement firm Kforce.com as well as computerjobs.com. Regardless of whether you are already in the Internet and technology industry or are looking to break through, this is the guide for you!

OneHourWiz: Stock Options
By Vivian Wagner, ISBN: 1587621053
Stock options are being granted to record numbers of employees, but many people receiving stock options don't really understand what they are. This guide gives you the information you need to make informed decisions about stock options, including how to value them and your company, the difference between Incentive Stock Options (ISOs) and Nonqualified Stock Options (NQSOs), the tax consequences of exercising your options, as well as information for those who want to get into options trading on their own-in an easy to understand language and format. This OneHourWiz guide also includes interviews with noted experts in the field, lawyers from some of the top law firms in the world, CFOs from companies such as Hoovers, LifeMinders,

Register.com, a sample stock option plan from Intel, and worksheets to help you keep track of your stock options.

OneHourWiz: Landing Your First Job
By Andrew Goldsmith, ISBN: 1587620253
Are you a college senior terrified to graduate? Or a freshman with a lot of foresight? This is the guide you need to make sure your first step into the real world takes you in the right direction (and to start thinking ahead to that second step!). You'll get advice from the director of Career Services at one of the hottest Ivy League schools in the country and advice from such experts as the head of recruiting from PriceWaterhouseCoopers. You'll read the stories of people who just a few years ago were standing exactly where you are, and are now establishing themselves at dotcoms, consulting firms, finance jobs, and even in the publishing, entertainment and theater scenes!

OneHourWiz: Public Speaking
By Sporty King, ISBN: 1587621096
OneHourWiz: Public Speaking can help anyone master the art of public speaking. Whether giving a presentation to a few individuals, presenting to thousands of people, or just wanting to speak more confidently to others, this guide will give you all of the keys to success as a public speaker in an easy to understand format and language. This proprietary process used to become a public speaker employed by Sporty King, a renowned public speaker, is sure to get you speaking confidently in no time.

New Titles Available Every Month!

Visit Your Local Bookseller Today!

Visit www.OneHourWiz.com for a Complete List of Titles

OneHourWiz™
Stock Options

Core Area 1: The 10 Most Important Principles 15

1. Read this Book 15
2. Know the Terms 15
3. Know Your Options 15
4. Talk to Your Human Resources Manager 15
5. Read the Fine Print 15
6. Exercise Carefully 15
7. Understand the Value of Your Options 16
8. The Tax Man Cometh 16
9. Diversify 16
10. See an Accountant and/or Tax Lawyer 16

Core Area 2: Background Information 17

Employee Stock Options 17
Evaluating Your Stock Options Benefits Package 19
Valuing Your Options and Your Company 20
Diversifying Your Portfolio 21
Stock Options in a Down Market 22
Options Trading 23

Core Area 3: Focal Points 24

Understanding the Language of Stock Options 24
Alternative Minimum Tax (AMT) 24
Basis 25
Capital Gain/Capital Loss 26
Compensation Income 26
Exercise 26

Fair Market Value 27
Holding Period 27
In the Money/Out of the Money 27
Reload Options 28
Spread 28
Strike Price 28
Vested 28
Nonqualified Stock Options (NQSOs) 29
Who Gets NQSOs 29
Basic Tax Rules 30
Exercising NQSOs 31
Public vs. Private Companies 32
Incentive Stock Options (ISOs) 34
Holding Period 35
Alternative Minimum Tax 36
When Your ISO Stock Matures 39
$100,000 Limitation and Vesting Schedules 39
Exercising Your Options 40
How to Exercise 41
When to Exercise 42
NQSOs vs. ISOs 43
Bear Market Blues 44
What to Do After Exercising 46
Taxes 46
NQSOs vs. ISOs 47
Income Tax 47
Alternative Minimum Tax 48
Capital Gains and Losses 50
Gift and Estate Tax 53
Estimated Taxes 54
Options Trading 55
How Options Trading Works 56
American vs. European-style Options 58
Valuing Stock Options 58

Taxes 59
Options Strategy 60

Core Area 4: Interviews With Industry Visionaries 63
Christopher J. Loiacono, C.P.A., Richard A. Eisner & Company 63
Debra Brian, Director of Worldwide Compensation and Benefits, Intel Corporation 77

Core Area 5: Excerpts from Experienced Individuals 84
Mark I. Gruhin 84
The Ups and Downs of Stock Options 84
Arnold Levine 85
Tax Consequences of Stock Options 85
Stock Option Misperceptions 86
James Hutchinson 88
Understanding Stock Options 88
Vesting Trends 88
Tim Bixby 89
What to Look for in an Internet Company 89
David R. Henkel 90
Internet Companies and Stock Options 90
Public vs. Private Companies 91
What Employees Need to Understand about Finance 92
Negotiating a Fair Compensation Package 93
Joan Platt 94
Stock Options as Recruiting Tool: Then and Now 94
Public vs. Private Companies 95
Mary Dridi 95
The Benefits of Stock Options 95
What to Look for Regarding a Company's Finances 97

Core Area 6: Case Studies & Worksheets **99**
Case Study: Intel Corporation, 1997 Stock Option Plan 99
Worksheets 117
Figuring Value 118
Vesting Schedule 119

Core Area 7: Resources for Further Research **120**
Recommended Books 120
Recommended Websites 122
Bibliography 122

Core Area 8: Key Words Glossary **125**

Core Area 1

The 10 Most Important Principles

So you want to become a OneHourWiz with stock options? You've come to the right place. Here are ten steps that you'll want to follow:

1. Read this Book: It has information, analysis, helpful hints, interviews, and sample documents to move you along the path of "wiz-dom."

2. Know the Terms: Stock options, like many other financial matters, come complete with a whole new language: strike price, vesting, exercising. Learning the language will help you to understand what you're doing.

3. Know Your Options: Do you have ISOs or NQSOs? Know what you have and why it matters.

4. Talk to Your Human Resources Manager: Find out exactly what kind of stock option program your company offers, and how you can benefit.

5. Read the Fine Print: If you have a stock option agreement or contract from your employer, read it. You'll be surprised how much you can learn from this document.

6. Exercise Carefully: Know how and when to exercise your options.

7. Understand the Value of Your Options: Whether you work for a private or a public company, you'll need to learn how to value your options.

8. The Tax Man Cometh: Don't forget to pay what you owe, when you owe it.

9. Diversify: Even if you like your company, you don't want all of your investments tied up with it in options. A prolonged downturn in the market may hit you particularly hard if all of your eggs are in one basket.

10. See an Accountant and/or Tax Lawyer: Reading a book is no substitute for getting advice from an actual person, particularly since everyone's case is unique-especially if you are talking about the potential for a lot of money. Reading this book will give you a great head start on options, but think about asking your accountant or tax lawyer some additional questions next time you pay them a visit.

Core Area 2

Background Information

A stock option is, essentially, the option to buy a stock at a future date for a specified price. Most people are introduced to stock options through benefits packages offered by their employers, but you can also buy and sell options on your own, as well.

Although investing in stocks is relatively easy to understand – you buy shares in a company, and these shares can go up or down in value according to that company's growth and profits and the overall mood of the market itself – options investing is a somewhat more complicated matter. This chapter gives an introduction to some of the basic concepts on which the following chapters expand.

Employee Stock Options

Stock options have become increasingly popular as a form of equity compensation through employee stock option plans – and they're not just for CEOs and other bigwigs anymore, but for people at all levels of a company. The National Center for Employee Ownership, based in Oakland, California, estimates that somewhere between 7 million and 10 million employees, working for 4,000 different companies, are included in some form of stock option plans. These numbers are staggering, especially when you consider the fact that many of these employees aren't sure what they're receiving when they receive stock options, and don't know what to do with them after they receive them. Information and advice can be hard to come by, and yet if you're one of these employees it's vital to become as fully informed as possible, since your stock options may be a significant part of your overall compensation package.

Companies offer options to their employees as a way of inducing employee loyalty and involving their employees in the "big picture" of the company's performance in the stock market.

When you receive a stock option grant, you have the option of purchasing a specific number of shares of the stock at a future date (called exercising your options) for a specified price (called the strike price); if the stock has gone up in value, your option is "in the money," and you stand to make money. If it has gone down in value, your option is "out of the money"; you won't gain anything, but technically you won't lose money, since you aren't required to purchase the stock. Your exercise price is likely to be set at the price of the stock at the time you receive the stock option grant.

You can exercise your options when they become vested – that point when your contract specifies you can purchase the stock. This may be immediately, or it may be delayed for one or more years after you receive the stock option grant. Delayed vesting periods tend to induce company loyalty, since you have a reason to stick with a company for a while to hopefully reap the rewards of the growth of the company by exercising your stock options at a later date.

Here's how it might work: your employer gives you the option of buying 2,000 shares of your company at $15 a share in one year from the date of the grant. At that point, the stock is selling for $20 a share, and you decide to exercise your options. You must come up with $30,000 to buy the stock, which is now worth $40,000. You can then turn around and sell the stock and pocket your $10,000 profit, or you might decide to hold onto it. To purchase the stock, you can come up with the cash, borrow the money, use stock you already own to complete the transaction, or participate in what is called a cashless exercise, in which you work with your employer to buy and sell the stock immediately.

There are primarily two different kinds of stock options that you can get from an employer: nonqualified stock options and incentive stock options. Receiving and exercising these different stock options have various tax consequences, and this book goes through the tax side of stock options in detail. Just remember, at some point in the stock option game you will most likely owe some kind of tax, and you'll need to keep on top of it. Read this book, and consult with a tax preparer or tax attorney to make sure that you're giving Uncle Sam his due.

Evaluating Your Stock Options Benefits Package

When you get a job offer with a company, you'll want to find out as much as you can about the entire benefits package, which could include anything from health and life insurance to a company car. If that package includes stock options, you'll want to pay special attention to the specifics of the stock option plan. Your employer may offer stock options as a part of your overall compensation; for example, a $60,000 yearly (cash) income plus stock options that are potentially worth $15,000 or more each year could together compose a $75,000 salary.

On the other hand, you and your employer might consider the stock options to be an addition to your regular income compensation – sort of the frosting on the cake. In this case, you'll be offered what you're worth in terms of salary, and stock options will be thrown in to sweeten the deal. It might not be clear what kind of offer you're receiving, or it might hinge on your judgment of your own worth on the labor market, but it's important that you consider the overall framework in which you're receiving the options.

When you are offered stock options by a company, you'll probably be offered an option agreement, specifying the major points regarding the kinds of options you're being offered, how many shares you're being offered, their exercise price, the schedule by which you can exercise these options, and any other limitations, exclusions, or special considerations. You'll want to read the fine print of this document carefully, and if you have any questions, talk to your company's human resources manager or the person within your organization who is in charge of the employee stock option package. You might also want to get an accountant or attorney to look at the agreement with you to see if it's favorable to you.

The stock option agreement will likely be the only document that you're given at the outset, but behind this document is the company's stock option plan – a more detailed and thorough document that has been designed by the company's board of directors and most likely approved by the company's shareholders. The stock option plan specifies how many stock option shares, and what kinds of stock options, will be available to employees, along with other pertinent information. You'll probably want to request a copy of the plan so that you can get an overall picture of the company's stock option offerings, and how you fit into this larger picture.

Valuing Your Options and Your Company

It's relatively easy to know the value of your company if it's a publicly traded one. You can simply check the daily value of the company's stock and get a good idea of its current fair market value. This doesn't ensure that the future price of the stock will be more than what it is today; in fact, one of the major risks of stock option grants is that the underlying stock will go down in value, thus rendering your options essentially worthless. That, however, is the risk you take – and you hope when you receive options that the value of the stock will go up. At least you will have a clear idea what your options are worth – or not worth – on any given day.

If your company is a privately held one, however, judging the value of its stock options can be trickier. Basically, you're going to have to find out what the fair market value of that stock is – or what it could be once the company goes public. This will mean asking a manager in your company what the value of its stock is estimated to be. This might be based on a transaction in which some of the company's stock was sold to a third-party. The company might also assign value to the stock based on its own evaluation of its worth and its potential initial public offering price; or it might hire a valuation firm that provides it with a valuation report on the company and its stock. In any scenario, you'll need to be especially cautious if you receive stock options from a privately held company, since the value of these options is at best unpredictable and at worst seemingly arbitrary.

Diversifying Your Portfolio

Although it's tempting if you work for a company that grants stock options to load up on company stock as you exercise these options, you'll want to adhere to principles of diversification just as if you were investing in stock on your own, separately from any employee benefits package. Diversification is the spreading out of your investments across various stocks and other investment instruments, thus reducing the risk that you take from putting all of your eggs in one basket. No matter how good your company's stock is doing – and how excited you are about the future growth of your company – you'll want to ensure that you have a diversified portfolio.

How do you achieve this, and yet still take advantage of your company's option plan? Perhaps the easiest way is to exercise your options – buy your company's stock – then sell at least some of this stock when market conditions are favorable and use this cash to purchase stock in other companies. This lets you take advantage of your options plan and yet at the same time spread out your investment risk. As later chapters in this book emphasize, exercising options and selling stock may generate tax consequences, so you'll want to make sure that these consequences don't outweigh any diversification benefits you'll receive by selling the stock. Whatever you end up doing, it's a good idea to regularly review your portfolio and attempt to achieve at least some degree of diversification.

Stock Options in a Down Market

Stock option grants were a particularly popular form of compensation during the late 1990s, when the stock market reached stratospheric heights, particularly in the tech sector. During this time, many instant millionaires were born in the Silicon Valley – stock and stock option grants helped to make them rich on paper.

With a potentially rocky market in 2001 and beyond, stock options might become less popular – particularly if tech companies and the value of their stock continue to falter. If you receive stock options from your employer during a turbulent market, it's even more important to be aware of when to exercise, how to exercise, and how to avoid negative tax consequences.

Down markets can wreck havoc with your carefully laid financial plans, including any benefits package you receive that includes stock options as a major part. You just might end up with stock options that are worthless, which eats away at your overall compensation. During down markets or markets that seem to be threatening to turn down – or if your company's stock seems to be hitting the skids despite what the overall market is doing – you'll probably want to make sure that any stock option grants that you receive are in addition to your regular compensation, not a substitute for cash compensation.

Options Trading

In addition to receiving stock options as a form of equity compensation, you can also buy and sell options on your own in the options market. These are similar to stock options that are part of employee benefits packages, but they do have their own set of rules and tax consequences. Although this book focuses primarily on stock option grants from employers, it does introduce some of the details about options trading. If you want to get into options trading – which can be a fun and valuable part of your portfolio – check out some of the details in the last section of Core Area 3.

Core Area 3

Focal Points

I. Understanding the Language of Stock Options

One of the most difficult things about stock options is that they have their own language. If you don't understand this language, you may be in the dark about some important factors that are going to influence you and possibly your financial outlook.

There is a key words glossary at the end of the book, but before you begin reading the book, it's important to understand some of the following basic concepts:

Alternative Minimum Tax (AMT)

The Alternative Minimum Tax (AMT) is a federal tax that you may owe when you exercise an incentive stock option (ISO). It is not an income tax *per se*; it was started as a way to tax the money that people receive that isn't classified as "income." AMT liability affects people who get money from a variety of sources, including the exercise of incentive stock options. In terms of its application to stock options, this tax is figured according to the spread that exists on the day you exercise an ISO – in other words, the day you buy the underlying stock. It may also affect you if you have significant long-term capital gains from ISOs or traditional stock purchases. AMT liability is figured by computing your taxes according to an alternative set of rules, and then comparing these taxes with what you would pay under regular income tax rules; the higher liability will be yours. The alternative set of rules used to figure AMT excludes deductions for personal exemptions, some medical expenses, and state and local taxes; importantly, it also factors in the income from exercising incentive stock options and long-term capital gains. This income is factored in by reporting an AMT adjustment when you file your taxes. Basically, you'll be adjusting your income to reflect the forms of income that might otherwise not have been taxed.

Basis

For the purposes of figuring capital gains taxes, essentially your basis is where you start with a stock or other investment. If you buy 500 shares of a stock for $10 a piece, and at the same time pay $50 commission to a broker, your basis for this purchase would be $5,050 – or $10.10 per share – which includes the price of the stock plus the commission. Figuring the basis for options can be slightly different, but it is based on the same principle. When determining your basis for exercising nonqualified stock options (NQSOs), for instance, your basis equals the amount you paid for the stock plus the income you report at the time of exercise (in other words, your basis is the fair market value of the stock). There are many elements that affect how you will figure your basis, and it is rarely a simple process. Your basis is a very important number, however, since it will be used to figure the taxes you owe. You can also have what is called a "dual basis." When you exercise incentive stock options, AMT can create a dual basis for you in the stock that you purchase through an exercise; you will have one basis for the purposes of regular income tax and another for the purposes of AMT.

Capital Gain/Capital Loss

Capital gains are the income that you earn when you sell a capital asset – which can be anything other than products that you sell as part of a business – that has appreciated in value. A capital loss comes when you sell a capital asset that has depreciated in value; in other words, you sell it for less than the amount for which you purchased it. Depending on the type of stock options you have, how long you hold the stock after exercising your options, and other miscellaneous rules surrounding the options, you may have a capital gain or loss when you sell the stock that you receive from exercising stock options.

Compensation Income

Compensation income is considered "ordinary income," i.e., money that you earn for being employed by a company. You can earn compensation income either as a regular employee or an independent contractor, and when you exercise nonqualified stock options (NQSOs) you will need to report the difference between the exercise price and the fair market value of the stock as compensation income. If you're a regular employee, your company will report this income to you along with the rest of your income. If you're an independent contractor, you'll need to keep careful records of all income earned through the exercise of NQSOs.

Exercise

When you purchase stock from an option grant, it is called "exercising" the options. You will exercise your options at a pre-determined price, called the "strike price," which will have been spelled out in your option agreement. You will only want to exercise your options if and when they are worth something – meaning that the exercise price is lower than the fair market value of the stock (see below). If your exercise price is higher than the fair market value, your options are essentially worthless. There are a number of different ways of exercising your options. You may pay cash for the stock, which means you have to have all of the money available for the purchase (and for any taxes) at the time of exercise. If you don't have the cash, your employer might have an arrangement available with a broker to let you have a "cashless exercise," meaning that you don't need any cash at the time of exercise. In this case you typically will purchase the stock and then sell it immediately, pocketing the difference. Some people take out a loan (either from a broker or a third party) to do essentially the same thing as a cashless exercise, and others may be able to use stock they already own to exercise more options.

Fair Market Value

Fair market value is the price of a stock on the stock exchange at a given time on a given day. If the stock is not publicly traded, fair market value is determined by other methods, including internal evaluation methods of a company or the evaluation of a third party evaluator.

Holding Period

If you exercise incentive stock options (ISOs), you will receive favorable tax treatment on the exercise if you hold the options for more than one year from the date of exercise or more than two years from the date of the granting of the options. Note that this means a year (or two) plus at least one day. This time period is called the holding period. If you exercise the options before the holding period is up, it is called an "early disposition."

In the Money/Out of the Money

Your stock options are considered "in the money" if the underlying stock is worth more than the exercise price. They are called "out of the money" (or "underwater") if the stock is worth less than the exercise price. In this case, options are essentially worthless.

Reload Options

Also sometimes known as restoration or replacement options, reload options are options you can receive by turning in shares of stock that you already own. This method of obtaining options is only available if your company specifies that it allows for it. Reload options are beneficial in that they let you cash in on the money for your options when they are in the money, and lock in new options that allow for the potential of even greater profits.

Spread

The spread is the difference between an option's exercise price and the fair market value of the stock. The spread is used to figure income, basis, and other key numbers on your exercise. It may also affect when you decide to exercise your options, since you might want to wait until there is a large spread between the exercise price and the value of the stock.

Strike Price

The strike price is the price at which your options are fixed when they are granted to you; it is also the price at which you can exercise the options, or the exercise price.

Vested

Your options are vested, essentially, when you are allowed to exercise them. Your company may establish a "vesting schedule," which grants you options at a particular strike price, but then has a timetable according to which you can exercise them. The underlying stock upon which options are based can also be vested –

meaning that there may be a timetable according to which you can or cannot sell this stock, even after you have exercised your options. Vesting schedules are often tied to what is called a "substantial risk of forfeiture," which limits your ability to exercise options according to how long you work for the company, a promise not to work for a competing company upon quitting your current job, or other factors. If, for instance, you leave the company before your vesting schedule is up, you may forfeit your right to the options or the stock that you purchase when you exercise the options, or you may have to sell the stock back for less than its fair market value.

II. Nonqualified Stock Options (NQSOs)

Nonqualified stock options (NQSOs), also sometimes called nonstatutory stock options, are the most common kind of stock options that are granted to employees. NQSOs get their name from the fact that unlike incentive stock options, or ISOs (also called qualified stock options), NQSOs do not qualify for special tax treatment with the IRS. You will know that you have nonqualified stock options if your agreement specifies them as such; look at the first paragraph or opening page of your agreement for this information.

Who Gets NQSOs

NQSOs are available both to employees and non-employees. As far as employees are concerned, companies will often offer NQSOs to people in non-managerial positions, saving ISOs as a special benefit for managers and other executives. Because of a $100,000 limitation on ISOs, however – meaning that companies can only grant ISOs worth $100,000 annually to an employee – many managers and executives receive nonqualified stock options in addition to their ISOs, since $100,000 in stock options may not be enough to bring in the top candidates.

Companies can also offer NQSOs as a special reward to non-employees; if you are a non-employee (i.e., you're a consultant, freelance worker, independent contractor, non-employee director, or other affiliate of a company and you do not have taxes withheld from your paycheck and you do not receive a W-2), NQSOs are the *only* kind of options you can receive from a company. During the late 1990s with the rise of start-up Internet companies – many of which rely heavily on the use of freelance workers and independent contractors – NQSOs became a popular way to pay such workers either in part or sometimes, though rarely, in full.

If you're an employee, you will most likely see your income from the exercise of any NQSOs reported as income on your W-2 at the end of the year. If you're a non-employee, you'll need to keep careful records on your own of all of your income, including any that comes from the exercise of NQSOs.

Basic Tax Rules

The basic thing to remember about the tax implications of NQSOs is that though you do not owe taxes when they are granted, you will owe regular income taxes on your gains for the year in which you exercise them. This income is figured by determining the difference – also called the spread – between the strike or exercise price and the stock's current value when you exercise. In addition to this income tax, you may also owe capital gains taxes on the stock when you sell it.

In other words, if you exercise 500 options that have a strike price of $9, and when you exercise them the stock is worth $11, you will have to report $1,000 of income ($5,500 minus $4,500) and you must pay taxes – including income taxes, social security taxes, and Medicare taxes – on this amount just as you do on your salary or other income. After you exercise the options, the stock you own is treated just like any other stock in terms of taxes; you will owe capital gains taxes when you sell it. If you hold the stock for at least a year before selling it, you will pay long-term capital gains taxes of at most 20% on your gains; if you hold it less than a year, you'll owe short-term capital gains, which can be up to 39.6%.

When figuring taxes, you'll need to know what your basis is for the stock that you receive as part of exercising options. Essentially, the basis is the foundation stock price upon which your earnings or losses are built. When you buy stock through a broker, your basis will be the total amount of money that you spent to get that stock, including any fees that you paid to the broker. For NQSOs, however, your basis is determined by adding the price that you paid for the stock to the income you receive as part of the process of exercising your option. In other words, your basis is the fair market value of the stock at the time of your exercise.

Exercising NQSOs

When you exercise your NQSOs, you will have to report as compensation income the difference between the exercise price and the fair market value of the stock at the time you exercise. When deciding when to exercise your NQSOs, you'll need to consider when you want to receive (and pay taxes on) income and when you want to receive (and pay taxes on) capital gains. As you make these decisions, look at how your company's stock is doing and plan your exercising strategy accordingly.

One strategy for exercising NQSOs is to exercise them over several years (as allowed by your agreement, and before they expire) in order to spread out any income, thus perhaps keeping you from jumping into a higher tax bracket. Deferring taxes in this way is desirable for many people, but each individual situation varies.

One of the considerations when deciding when to exercise NQSOs is that when you exercise the options the money you receive will be considered compensation income, but after you exercise them any money you earn will be considered capital gain. Holding the stock that you receive as a result of the exercise for a year or less will result in your having to pay taxes on short-term capital gains. Holding it for longer than a year, however, will result in your paying taxes on long-term capital gains. Either way, once you've exercised the options you owe compensation taxes and you'll be looking at capital gains taxes in the future.

How consideration of capital gains affects the timing of your exercise of your NQSOs depends on your individual situation. If you're confident that the stock is growing rapidly, and you plan to hold onto the stock for over a year once you exercise, you may decide to exercise your NQSOs as early as possible. In this manner, you may owe less in compensation taxes than you would if you waited and the stock climbed in value, and you'll owe long-term capital gains taxes – which have rates that are lower than the rates for compensation income. You may, however, decide to wait to exercise for a longer period of time – perhaps until the options are about to expire. In this way, you will be deferring your payment of income tax, which in many situations can be beneficial.

Whenever you decide to exercise your NQSOs and whatever factors you take into account, one of the things that you'll have to weigh is compensation tax liability against potential capital gains tax liability. If you have questions about your specific situation, it never hurts to consult with a professional tax advisor.

Public vs. Private Companies

The value of your NQSOs is easy to determine if you work for a publicly traded company, which means a company that is traded on an established stock exchange. Just check the value on any given day, compare this value with the exercise price spelled out in your option agreement, and you'll know the value of your options, and whether they are in or out of the money.

If you work for a company that is privately held, however – meaning that its stock is not traded on the stock exchange – figuring the value of your NQSOs is not such a simple process. You'll need to ask a representative of your company what the estimated value of the stock is, given the company's own evaluation, a third-party transaction, or a third-party evaluation process.

According to IRS Publication 525, which deals with the taxability of various employee benefits – including stock options – you can only determine the fair market value of an option from a privately held company if each of the following conditions exist: you can transfer the option; you can exercise the option immediately and in full; there are no conditions or restrictions that have a significant effect on the fair market value of the option, and the fair market value of the option privilege can be readily determined. If the above conditions do not apply, you also won't be able to exercise the options, since with NQSOs you won't owe any taxes until the options are exercisable. In other words, in terms of taxes you don't have to worry about the value of your options until you exercise them, and at that point the fair market value of those options is necessarily clear.

You may, however, be curious about the potential value of your options, particularly since they are part of your compensation package and you probably have a great deal of hope invested in them. For this reason, it makes sense to find out from your company the estimated value of these options – and also to keep an eye on the market to see how the stock of similar companies is faring.

As the above discussion suggests, if you work for a privately held company you'll want to consult with a tax advisor who can help you to work through valuation issues and determine the taxes that you'll owe when you do exercise the options.

III. Incentive Stock Options (ISOs)

Incentive stock options (ISOs) get their name from the fact that they give employees an incentive to stick with a company and make that company profitable. They are part of a category of options called statutory stock options by the IRS; in addition to ISOs, this category includes options granted under employee stock purchase plans. ISOs are also sometimes called qualified stock options, so named because they are qualified to receive special tax treatment by the IRS.

When you exercise ISOs, you generally won't owe compensation taxes on the money you earn from exercise. Unlike nonqualified stock options, when you exercise incentive stock options and abide by a special holding period, you won't be required to report compensation income. Because of this special tax treatment, you may make more money in the long run with ISOs – but only if you understand and follow all of the rules. To get the full tax benefits of these options, you must hold the stock that you purchase for more than one year from the date of exercise and more than two years from the date the options were granted. You might be tempted to sell the stock before then to cash in on your earnings and cover the cost of the exercise, but if you do so the options will lose their special tax status and possibly subject you to higher taxes than if you are patient.

Unlike NQSOs, ISOs have to be issued with a strike price equal to or greater than the existing fair market value of the underlying stock. ISOs are available only to employees; non-employees and other people affiliated with a company can only get nonqualified stock options. ISOs have traditionally been reserved for people with some stature in a company – CEOs, high-level managers, and others. They are becoming increasingly popular, however, and companies are beginning to offer ISOs as a benefit even for those lower on the corporate food chain.

Holding Period

To get the full benefits of the special tax treatment that is available for ISOs, you'll need to abide by a holding period. Any tax on your earnings will be deferred until you sell the stock – and the length of time for which you hold onto the stock will determine whether or not you get special tax treatment. If you hold onto the stock for more than one year from the day you exercise it, and more than two years from the day the option was granted, you'll owe only long-term capital gains taxes on the money that you have gained – in other words, the difference between the amount of money you paid for the stock or the exercise price and the amount you receive when you ultimately sell the stock.

The fact that you will owe capital gains taxes on your earnings instead of regular income tax is a definite tax benefit. The top rates on long-term capital gains taxes are currently topped at 20%, as opposed to 39.6% for regular federal income tax; holding onto the stock you get from ISOs for the holding period can thus be a smart move, giving you a significant tax benefit.

If you don't hold onto the stock for the full length of the holding period, however, your tax status will be the same as if you had nonqualified options; this early sale of your stock from an ISO is called a "disqualifying disposition" or "early disposition." In this case, you'll have to pay income taxes on the stock as of the day of exercise, in addition to capital gains taxes when you sell the stock, if it has appreciated.

According to IRS Publication 525, which deals among other things with the tax consequences of employee stock options, you must report the gain you receive from the exercise of an ISO as ordinary income "up to the amount by which the stock's fair market value exceeded the option price when you exercised the option." In other words, you must pay income taxes on the spread between the fair market value and the exercise price at the point of exercise if you don't meet the holding period requirements. If you sell the stock several months after the date of exercise – before the holding period is up – you will owe regular income taxes on the spread at the date of exercise, and short-term capital gains on any excess gain. If when you sell the stock you have a loss, it is a short-term capital loss, and you will not need to report any ordinary income.

Here's an example of how this might work. Your company grants you ISOs on July 1, 1998, allowing you to buy 500 shares of its stock at $5 a share. You exercise the options on February 1, 1999 at a point when the options are selling on the open market for $10 a share. On February 2, 2000, you sell the stock for $12 a share. In this scenario, you held the stock for over a year from the date of exercise, but you did not hold it for more than two years from the date the options were granted. Thus, for the year 2000, you'll need to report as compensation income the difference between the option price, which was $5, and the stock's value when you exercised that option, which was $10. The remaining gain will be treated as capital gain. In other words, the selling price when you sold the stock was $6,000. Your purchase price was $2,500, making your total gain $3,500. The amount you report as compensation for 2000 will be what you gained on the date of exercise – $2,500. You'll report the remaining $1,000 as capital gain.

Alternative Minimum Tax (AMT)

Although you can get away with paying no income tax on the exercising of ISOs, you may very well be hit by another tax: the

Alternative Minimum Tax, or AMT. The Alternative Minimum Tax is a parallel tax system in which the taxable income for individual taxpayers is recomputed after adding in items such as state and local taxes, real estate taxes, certain accelerated appreciation, and the spread that exists on incentive stock options. The spread that exists on the date of exercise for an ISO is added back when the Alternative Minimum Tax is computed. Depending on each individual situation, it's possible that if there's a significant spread, you might end up owing Alternative Minimum Tax when you exercise your ISOs.

As the IRS says in Publication 525, "For the alternative minimum tax, you must treat stock acquired through the exercise of an incentive stock option as if no special treatment applied. This means that, when your rights in the stock are transferable and no longer subject to a substantial risk of forfeiture, you must include as an adjustment in figuring alternative minimum taxable income the amount by which the fair market value of the stock exceeds the option price." In other words, AMT calculations take away the special tax treatment that is applied to the exercise of ISOs. When you figure AMT, you basically compare what you would owe under the two different tax structures, first by figuring your taxes normally (with the special treatment of the exercise of the ISOs) and then by figuring your taxes with the alternative rule structure of AMT. The larger of the two tax liabilities will be the one you owe.

AMT was started as a way of making sure that everyone pays taxes on income – even when it is not technically called "income." Most likely, when you exercise an ISO, you will owe AMT for the year of the exercise. Your AMT will be based on the amount of the spread when you exercise the stock, in other words, the difference between the price you pay for the stock and the market price of the stock at the time of your exercise (i.e., how much profit you make). AMT only kicks in, however, if you are still holding the stock at the end of the year. If you sell the stock before the end of the year, you can avoid AMT liability.

Basically, when you exercise an ISO you must report to the IRS what is called an "AMT adjustment"; this adjustment may or may not require you to pay AMT. When you file this adjustment, you create what is called a "dual basis" for your ISO stock. In regards to income taxes, your basis is simply what you paid for the stock when you exercised the options. For the AMT, however, your basis will be equal to the amount that you paid for the stock plus the AMT adjustment. In other words, consider the following scenario. Through the exercise of ISOs, you purchased 1000 shares of your company's stock for $25 when the fair market value of that stock was $50. Your total AMT adjustment for the purchase is $25 per share, for a total of $25,000. For the sake of regular taxes (either capital gain taxes or, if you don't abide by the holding period, compensation taxes), your basis would be $25. For the AMT, however, your basis would be $50.

There is a bright side to AMT. Through what is called the AMT credit, you might be able to get back in future years some of the money that you spent on AMT. You might be able to apply the AMT credit to the regular income tax that you pay in the years after you pay AMT, but you can only use the credit for years that you won't owe any AMT. There are special rules for figuring AMT credit, mostly based on the effects of timing on the taxes that you have owed through AMT. Based on working through these somewhat intricate rules, you might find that you can apply part, all, or none of a past year's AMT against a future year's regular income tax. Essentially, this credit carries forward into future years.

Because the rules surrounding AMT and the AMT credit are intricate, you'll want to consult a tax professional to understand how they apply in your situation. For more detailed information on this tax and how it may affect you, see the chapter on taxes later in this book

When Your ISO Stock Matures

The stock you receive from exercising an ISO option is considered mature when you have completed the full holding period. At this point, your gains will all be considered long-term capital gains, and not income. If you decide to sell the stock, you can do so with no more repercussions than if you were selling any other stock that you acquire. Remember: it's important that you fully evaluate your tax situation – and consult with a tax advisor – before deciding when and how to sell your mature ISO stock.

$100,000 Limitation and Vesting Schedules

There is also a limitation on the number of ISOs that can be granted to an employee in any given year; this limitation is referred to as the $100,000 limitation. A company can grant an employee ISOs that are exercisable into $100,000 of stock in any given year, with the price calculated on the date of grant.

For example, the current fair market value of a stock might be $2. A company can grant an employee ISOs that are exercisable in the first year into 50,000 shares of stock that are exercisable. Since that might not be enough to attract a top employee, the company might decide to string out the exercise dates over a number of years through vesting. So, the company can grant the employee 150,000 ISOs that are exercisable at $2, but divided into sets of 50,000 shares over three years. This kind of vesting schedule allows the company to attract top employees, without violating the $100,000 limitation rule. Because of the $100,000 limitation, high-level managers often get a mix of ISOs and NQSOs to make their stock option package larger and more attractive.

FOCAL POINTS

IV. Exercising Your Options

Exercising is the term used for the purchase of stock through an option grant. When you exercise, you'll be purchasing stock at a pre-determined price, called the "strike price," that is specified in your option agreement. Your agreement will also specify any exercising schedule and other terms – for example, how and when you can exercise your options. You'll want to read the fine print of your agreement carefully to see what kind of options you have, what the exercise price is, what the exercise schedule is, and whether you are receiving vested or nonvested stock.

It is common for stock option agreements to offer options that are exercisable over periods of 10 years or less. Typically, these are tied to a vesting schedule, meaning that certain numbers of options will be exercisable at certain times. For instance, 25% of your options might vest each year, and after four or five years all of your options might be vested. The options will have an expiration date – perhaps ten years in the future – beyond which you can no longer exercise them.

When you exercise, you might also receive either vested or nonvested stock. Vested stock is stock that you own with no strings attached. Nonvested stock is tied to special considerations, such as requiring you to work for the company for a period of time before you can sell the stock and make a profit.

With good fortune, when you're ready to exercise and your agreement allows you to do so, your options will be in the money, in other words, your strike price will be less than the fair market value of the stock. If this isn't the case, your options aren't worth anything, since you could buy the stock for less money on the open market; in this case, you'd do well to wait for the stock price to go up.

How to Exercise

There are several different ways that you can exercise your stock options when the time comes. How and when you exercise your options may or may not be written into your stock options agreement; review it carefully to discover any applicable rules. Your agreement may specify how and under what circumstances you can exercise your options. You'll also need to decide which and how many of your options to exercise. Once you've worked through the details and it's time to exercise, consult with your human resources manager and tell him or her what you are planning to do.

Exercising options is, basically, buying shares of the stock upon which your options are based. Thus, when you exercise your options, you're going to have to decide how to pay for these shares of stock.

Here are some typical methods of payment; you can choose one or a combination of the following, depending on your circumstances:

- **Cash**

The simplest and most traditional way of exercising your options is to pay cash for them. Although it is still a popular choice for many people, this method may be difficult or impossible if you don't have enough funds to purchase the stock up front.

- **Cashless exercise**

In a cashless exercise, you sell the stock that you purchase immediately; the selling price covers the cost of the stock and you pocket the difference. This typically requires that your company have a special arrangement with a broker to carry out this form of payment.

- **Loan**

  Another option is to get a loan – either from a broker or from a third party – to pay for the exercise; you can then immediately sell the stock and pay off the loan.

- **Stock**

  An increasingly popular way to exercise stock options is to swap stock that you have to cover the price of exercising. With this method, you can turn in shares of stock that are worth the equivalent of the cash price for the option. There are tax benefits to this kind of exercise, and it is convenient because you won't need to come up with cash for the exercise. Though you won't need cash to exercise the option with this method, you may still need cash to pay for any tax liabilities.

When to Exercise

Deciding when to exercise your options can be just as important as how you exercise them. The timing of your exercise can have an impact on the profit you make and also on the taxes that you owe, so it's important that you know the best time for exercising your options.

When you exercise your options may be determined in part by the fine print of your options agreement, so you'll want to read that carefully and talk to your human resources department if you have any questions. Then, you'll want to consult with your tax preparer or accountant to figure out what the tax consequences will be for various exercising times and strategies.

There are basically three choices involved when deciding when to exercise your options. You might decide to exercise your options as soon as you are allowed to do so; this will work particularly well if you think the stock is priced well at the date you can first exercise.

You can also exercise your options gradually, thus dollar-cost averaging your way into the stock. This can be a good idea if you want to take advantage of a range of stock prices, thus evening out not just the value of the stock you purchase but also potentially your tax liability. If you're planning on selling some of the stock and investing in other companies and industries, this strategy also allows you to dollar-cost average into the market as a whole.

Finally, you can wait for as long as your agreement allows you to wait to see if the stock goes up in value. Your choices about when to exercise will be limited by what your particular agreement says – including your vesting schedule, the expiration of the options, how long you work for the company, and other limitations – so you'll want to check the details of your agreement before you take any action.

Generally, it's a good bet to keep your stock options right up until they are just about to expire, so that you can let the stock price increase as much as possible – although this assumes that the market (and the particular stock) is headed steadily up. If you're planning on selling your options immediately upon exercise, it's good to wait until you think the stock price has reached a peak. Selling will then let you cash in on your profit without worrying about whether the stock will plunge right after you buy it.

NQSOs vs. ISOs

The kind of stock options you have will probably influence your decision about when to exercise them. If you have NQSOs, the exercise will be considered compensation income for tax purposes, and you might therefore decide to exercise the options gradually in order to spread the income out – and not push you into a higher tax bracket for a particular year. This strategy may let you defer some of your taxes until a later date.

Likewise, AMT considerations might affect when you exercise your ISOs. A gradual exercise can be wise in this case as well, since you might be able to exercise a few of your options each year without triggering AMT liability. ISOs have the added provision of a holding period for the stock of either one year from the date of exercise or two years from the date you were granted the ISOs if you want to receive favorable tax treatment on the sale of the stock. When considering this holding period, therefore, you might decide to exercise your ISOs as soon as possible so that you can sell the stock in a year.

Bear Market Blues

In a down market or even a bear market, stock options are likely to be a less popular benefit than they are in a bull market. If the market is headed south and taking your company's stock with it, your options could become out of the money – meaning that you could end up never exercising them at all because they are worthless. In down markets, therefore, stock options become less attractive as a substitute for compensation. They generally will continue to be offered as an employee benefit, but they aren't as much a substitute for compensation as they are an added benefit – one that people realize could turn out to be worth nothing at all.

Downturns in the market can be particularly dangerous if you borrow money to exercise options, and then the stock immediately plunges – leaving you not only with stock that has gone down in value but also with unwanted debt. You might also end up exercising your options at a peak, hold onto the stock, and then watch the stock plummet in value. This happened to many people in the year 2000, as the market – especially tech stocks – plunged, leaving many people who had exercised their options early in the year looking at significant losses. Worse yet, many of them also owed back-breaking sums of AMT or income tax on the "profit" they had gained at the time of exercising, despite the fact that that profit had disappeared by the end of the year.

Exercising options is a tricky business. As with most other forms of investing, there's no guarantee that you're going to make money and there's even the possibility that you might lose some. You'll want, therefore, to think not just about when to exercise your options, but when to sell your stock. As always, it's wise to consult with an accountant about your particular situation. Watch the market, and watch your own company's stock. Certainly, you can't predict fluctuations in stock price or a downturn in the market, but you can be cautious and make sure that you're prepared for the worst.

One choice that you have if you are working for a company during the course of a serious market downturn or correction – and consequently are loaded up with a number of worthless options – is to look for another job. While it seems a drastic move, the benefit is that with a new job you might get new options, and ones that are priced according to the current level of the market. In this scenario, you will benefit more from the eventual rebound in the market than you would have at your old job. It's a way of getting in on the bottom of stock prices; just as regular investors "buy low," employees looking for attractive options packages might find their best deals in a down market. The only catch is that you have to be willing to change jobs, and there are certainly downsides to this strategy – particularly if you've only worked for a short time at your job and still need to gain experience and seniority there.

Some companies also offer employees new stock options on a continual basis, so you might be able to get more attractively priced options if you stick it out with the company you're with.

What to Do After Exercising

After exercising options, you'll own stock in your company, and you'll therefore have choices to make about what to with this stock. Should you hold it or sell it? For NQSOs, you're going to owe compensation income tax on the exercise – so you might decide to sell the stock immediately so that you can make a profit, pay back your exercise price, and/or make sure that you have enough money to cover the taxes. For ISOs, you have an incentive to hold the stock for more than a year from the date of exercise and more than two years from the date of the option grant so that you won't owe compensation.

If you work for a publicly traded company, you have more choices about what to do with your stock than if you work for a private company. If you've exercised options from a private company, you'll probably have to wait to sell your stock for a profit until the company has an initial public offering or is sold to another, publicly traded company. Until then, you have stock that might be worth something, but does not have a buyer.

V. Taxes

Taxes are one of the most important – and one of the least understood – factors when it comes to making the most of your stock options. Since every situation is unique, it's a good idea to consult with an accountant about what taxes you will owe as a result of exercising stock options. What kind of options you have, when you exercise them, and other factors will come into play in determining your tax liability.

NQSOs vs. ISOs

As mentioned before, you won't owe taxes when nonqualified stock options (NQSOs) are granted, but you will owe regular income taxes on your gains for the year in which you exercise them. Your income for the purposes of taxes is determined by figuring the spread between the strike or exercise price and the stock's fair market value at the time of exercise. In addition to this income tax, you may owe capital gains taxes on the stock when you sell it.

With incentive stock options (ISOs), when you exercise the options and abide by a special holding period, you won't be required to report compensation income. You may, however, be liable for the Alternative Minimum Tax, which is discussed in detail below.

It's vital for the purposes of tax computation that you know what kind of stock options you have. Generally, you can find this information in the fine print of your stock option agreement. Read it, and if you still aren't sure, consult with an accountant or attorney.

Income Taxes

Income is money that you earn from a job or – if you're an independent contractor – from a client; you pay federal, state, and local income taxes on this income. When you exercise NQSOs, you will have to report as income the spread between the strike price of these options and the fair market value of the stock at the time of exercise.

Likewise, if you exercise ISOs but you don't then fulfill the holding period – which is the greater of one year from date of exercise or two years from the date of grant – these options will be treated as if they were nonqualified options and you will owe regular income taxes on the exercise of these options, as well.

Alternative Minimum Tax

The Alternative Minimum Tax (AMT) was started as a way to make sure that even wealthy people with lots of tax loopholes would have to pay taxes on much of their income. It gets its name from the fact that the government thought it a wise idea to ensure that everyone pays a minimum amount of taxes, if not through regular income tax then at least through this alternative, parallel tax system.

The tax, however, has raised a number of questions and complaints from people who feel they do not deserve to be burdened by this additional tax. Many people – not just those who consider themselves wealthy – find themselves subject to this tax. Though it's one of the least popular taxes, and it may eventually be changed or even eliminated, as of this writing it is still something that many of us will have to pay. To comply with the tax code, you must have at least a rudimentary understanding of this tax.

AMT affects a number of different kinds of income that otherwise might fly low under the radar, and one of these is the spread that exists when a person exercises incentive stock options. AMT, therefore, is something you'll need to deal with if you've been granted ISOs. It can also affect you if you have significant long-term capital gains from ISOs or traditional stock purchases.

In terms of its application to stock options, AMT liability is calculated according to the spread that exists on the date of exercise for an ISO. If you exercise an ISO, it is possible that you will owe AMT for the year of the exercise, but you might be able to avoid AMT liability if you sell the stock before the end of the year.

You'll want to understand both how to calculate your liability for AMT in a given year and also how to reduce your taxes in the years following this year through what is called the AMT credit.

Basically, AMT liability is figured by computing your taxes according to an alternative set of rules and then comparing these taxes with what you would pay under regular income tax rules; the higher liability is the one you will have. Among other things, this alternative set of rules does away with deductions for personal exemptions, some medical expenses, and state and local taxes, and it also factors in the income from exercising incentive stock options and from long-term capital gains. To factor in this income, you'll need to report what is called an AMT adjustment; in other words, you'll need to adjust your income to reflect these other forms of income.

To get a complete list of the rules for figuring AMT liability, consult with the IRS. If you complete your taxes with tax software, the software should be able to tell if you have AMT liability, and if you have your taxes done by an accountant, he or she will be able to figure it out for you. If you do your taxes by yourself, however, you'll have to fill out IRS Form 6251.

One important thing to understand about AMT is that it can create a *dual basis*. Just when you thought you understood what a basis was when it came to stock options, AMT can throw you a curveball. With typical stock purchases, your basis is going to equal the amount you paid for a stock (including broker's commissions). With nonqualified stock options, your basis will be the sum of money you paid to purchase a stock added to the sum of income that you receive from the exercise of the stock – which will most likely equal the fair market value of the stock. With incentive stock options, however, AMT can cause you to have a dual basis in the stock that you purchase through an exercise, with one basis for the purposes of regular income tax and another for the purposes of AMT.

In addition to affecting those who exercise ISOs, AMT also kicks in with large capital gains. If you sell the stock that you receive from exercising stock options, then you may be hit by AMT if you have a capital gain. A large capital gain, since it raises your income, can lower the degree to which the AMT exemption – meant to protect those with lower and middle incomes from owing AMT – will protect you. In other words, the AMT exemption will keep you from owing AMT if your income is below a certain level, but if you have significant capital gains in one year, you might very well be faced with AMT liability.

Luckily, thanks to what is called the AMT credit, even if you do have AMT liability for one year, you might be able to recover some or all of the tax you have paid in future years. If you do qualify for an AMT credit, you can apply this credit to your regular income in a future year or years. You might be able to receive the AMT credit for the exercise of incentive stock options if there is a timing issue: If you haven't sold the stock, and you wouldn't normally have been taxed on income that you haven't actually yet received, you might be able to receive an AMT credit in the year in which you finally sell the stock that you received from an exercise in a previous year. Unfortunately, the AMT credit may not be available to you if you had AMT because of a significant long-term capital gain, since this kind of gain is not considered by the IRS to be based on timing.

AMT is a complicated tax with many different factors and issues, and this section just gives you an overview. Each situation is different and will require individual attention, and as always with tax questions, it's best to consult with a tax attorney or accountant about your AMT liability and any possible AMT credits.

Capital Gains and Losses

Capital gains and losses refer to the money that you gain or lose when you sell a capital asset. Capital gains are the income that you earn when you sell a capital asset that has appreciated in value.

A capital loss occurs when you sell a capital asset that has depreciated in value. Because stocks are capital assets that can appreciate or depreciate, you could have a capital gain or loss when you sell stock that you received from exercising stock options.

There are two basic types of capital gains: short-term and long-term. Short-term capital gains are those that you incur through selling an asset that has appreciated and that you've held for one year or less. Short-term capital gains are subject to the same rates as regular income. Long-term capital gains are those you incur through selling an asset that you've held for longer than a year. The tax rates for long-term capital gains are much more attractive than those for short-term capital gains. The top rates on long-term capital gains are currently topped at 20%, as opposed to 39.6% for regular federal income tax. Thus, if you purchase a stock or other capital asset, it might make a lot of sense in terms of taxes to try to hold it for longer than a year before selling it. Recent changes in tax law also benefit some investors who hold their stock for longer than five years; check with the IRS or your tax advisor about whether these new rules apply to you.

Capital losses are also categorized as either short-term (based on the sale of an asset you've held for a year or less) or long-term (based on the sale of an asset you've held for more than a year). As you figure your taxes, you can deduct short-term capital losses from short-term capital gains, and long-term capital losses from long-term capital gains. If short-term loss exceeds the amount of short-term gain, you can also deduct the excess from long-term gain – or vice versa. If there is still capital loss left after you've done this math, you can deduct the loss from your regular income up to a $3,000 limit. Any amount of loss over this limit can carry over into the next year; at this point, you will treat it the same way as you would have treated it the previous year.

Capital losses, therefore, can eat away at your capital gains – a somewhat unfortunate circumstance considering the favorable tax rates that these capital gains would receive as opposed to your regular income.

To figure your capital gains, you'll also have to be able to understand what your basis is in a stock. Your basis is the base line from which profits or losses are determined. To figure your basis for the stock you purchase via nonqualified stock options (NQSOs) your basis will equal the amount you paid for the stock plus the income you report at the time of exercise. As discussed above, you can have a dual basis for ISOs – which means that your AMT adjustment may cause you to have a basis both for regular tax (based on the amount you paid for the stock plus the difference between that amount and the fair market value of the stock when you exercised the options) and a separate basis for AMT (based on an increase of this stock by the amount of your AMT adjustment).

When you file your taxes, Schedule D is the form on which you will show your capital gains or losses for a year. Paying attention to capital gains and losses will help you to make the most of your stock options and also to plan for the exercise of these options. Typically, it's a good idea to try to stay away from short-term gains, because they don't have the favorable tax treatment of long-term gains. Long-term losses, too, have their drawbacks. You might also want to defer taxes by putting off selling assets that have appreciated significantly; there is, in other words, a benefit to buying and holding, even when it comes to the stock you receive from stock options. If you pay attention to your basis, you can also try to sell those assets that have the highest basis, thus cutting down on your gains.

Gift and Estate Tax

Since the stocks that you receive through exercising employee stock options are assets that belong to your estate, it's important to consider the tax and other financial implications of gift and estate taxes on various transactions involving these stocks. You can transfer these stocks to members of your family or others, but you'll need to pay careful attention to the tax issues surrounding these gifts.

First, to avoid gift and estate tax, you can give cash or capital assets worth $10,000 per year per person. Thus, it's vital that you know the value of any assets that you transfer before you transfer them, particularly if you want to avoid hefty gift taxes. There is an exception for gifts made to your spouse, for which there is an unlimited exclusion from gift taxes.

Basically, if they are true gifts (i.e. not related to work or compensation in any way), the recipient does not owe any income tax for the gifts of stock or other assets. If these assets, however, continue to earn income after the point of gifting, the recipient will owe taxes on this income. Generally, basis and holding periods of capital assets that you give away will become the recipient's responsibility, but they will remain the same as when you owned these assets.

Transferring options instead of stock can be a little trickier. Although you can't transfer ISOs under any circumstance except death, you can give gifts of NQSOs. There are special tax rules regarding such transfers, however. If you give a gift of NQSOs to someone before the options have been exercised, then when those options are exercised you will be the one who owes taxes on that income – as if they still belonged to you. There are also special timing rules that apply to gifts of NQSOs. For instance, if you are required to work for your company for a specified period of time before you can exercise your options, any gift that you make of these options will not be considered complete for tax purposes until those options become exercisable. There are some benefits, though, to the transfer of NQSOs, since you might be able to save on gift and estate taxes in the future if you give rapidly appreciating options to someone now – given that you satisfy all timing and other IRS requirements.

Although this gives you an introduction, gift and estate planning are complicated matters, and you'll want to consult with a professional before giving away or transferring any stocks or options.

Estimated Taxes

If you owe too much money in taxes for a given year, you may owe a penalty to the IRS. To circumvent this – to ensure that you pay enough taxes throughout the year – you can either have more money withheld from your regular paycheck, or you can pay estimated quarterly tax payments.

The benefit of paying quarterly estimated taxes is that you'll be able to adjust the amount you pay each quarter based on any taxable events (exercising options or selling stocks or both) that happened in that quarter. Thus, if you have one particularly active quarter you'll be able to adjust your tax up; if you have a relatively non-eventful quarter, you can adjust down.

On the other hand, if you have all of your taxes taken out of your paycheck, you might find yourself having to file a new Form W-4 to adjust your withholding each month, a process which can be tedious at best and inaccurate at worst. If you realize at the end of the year that you're going to be behind in your tax payments, however, you can withhold significantly more taxes from your last paychecks of the year to cover the liability. The IRS doesn't care when you pay your withholding money; it assumes that any payments you make have been spaced out evenly throughout the year, even if you have bunched payments at the end of the year.

If you do decide to pay estimated tax payments, remember that they are due quarterly on the 15th of April, June, September, and January (of the next year). You must mail your payments by these dates for them to be considered on time. Request Form 1040-ES from the IRS, otherwise known as Estimated Tax Vouchers, and include these with your estimated tax payments. Once you pay estimated taxes one year, the IRS will send you the required forms automatically each year.

To figure how much to pay, you'll need to evaluate your income situation – either by yourself or with the help of a tax professional – and then make sure that you're paying over the course of the year at least 90% of your overall tax liability. Form 1040-ES includes a worksheet that can help you to calculate tax liability, but basically you'll want to look at your regular income, capital gains income, and other forms of income, apply the proper rates to each, and come up with a rough estimate of how much money you owe in taxes for that quarter. You want this estimate to be as accurate as possible, since if you pay too much you're cutting down on the of money you have for investing or other purposes, and if you pay too little you may end up owing a penalty after all.

Remember that if you keep records of all taxable events, including all stock option exercises, stock sales, and stock purchases, these records can be immensely valuable as you determine your estimated taxes. You'll also want to keep records of all the money that you send to the IRS for estimated tax payments.

VI. Options Trading

In addition to receiving stock options through your employer, you can also trade stock options on the open market – by buying and selling options contracts through a broker. This is a popular, fun but sometimes risky form of investing that isn't for everyone. If you're an experienced investor, however, and you're looking for a way to hedge your bets in the stock market, options trading might be for you.

Trading options on the market is different from receiving them from an employer, and there are differences in terminology. Some of the basic concepts, however, remain the same. This chapter provides you with a brief introduction to the fast-moving and complicated world of options trading; for more detailed information, see some of the books referenced at the end of this book.

Options were first officially traded in a standardized manner on April 26, 1973, when the Chicago Board Options Exchange (CBOE) opened. Since then, they have become tremendously popular. They are available through most brokers, and are traded daily in a manner very similar to the way stocks are traded. If you'd like to get into options trading, talk to your brokerage about its offerings, fees, and services for options trading.

How Options Trading Works

Just as they do when you receive them from an employer, stock options that you buy and sell on the market give you the option of purchasing (or selling) shares of a stock for a specified amount up to a date in the future when the option contract expires. They are also called "derivative securities," which means they derive their value from their underlying shares of stock. Traditional options contracts expire nine months from the date that they are first listed, but there are also longer options contracts called Long-term Equity Anticipation Securities (commonly known as LEAPS). LEAPS can expire as much as three years from the date the contract is listed. The expiration date for all stock options is the Saturday following the third Friday of the expiration month. For conventional options, the month is specified when you purchase the option; for LEAPS, the expiration month is always January of a specified year. At the point an option expires, the owner can get the difference between its strike price and the current price of the stock – but depending on the movement of the stock price, the option might also be worthless.

The price of an option is also known as its "premium"; this is the price that you pay for the option contract itself. The price of the underlying stock that the option contract specifies is known as the "strike price." Options contracts traditionally give you the right to buy or sell 100 shares of stock at a specified strike price.

In options terminology, a "call" gives you, as the owner of the option contract, the right to buy a stock at a specified price; a "put" allows you to sell a stock at a specified price. In neither case do you have any obligation to purchase the stock – only the right, and only then if you choose to exercise it. If you do choose to sell or buy the underlying stock upon which your options contract is based, it is called exercising the option – just as it is with employer-granted stock options.

In many cases in the world of options trading, however, options contract holders will not buy or sell the stock at all. Rather, they will resell either their call or their put options to interested buyers. To exercise either a call or a put option, you must file what is called an "exercise notice" through your broker or options trading firm before the option expires.

When you buy a call or put option, you have the right to buy or sell that underlying stock – and also the right to sell that option contract itself. When you sell that option, however, you have the obligation to sell or purchase that stock when you are "assigned" by the buyer. Being assigned means that you must fulfill the obligation that you sold when you sold the options contract. You will only be assigned, typically, if the option is in the money – or, in other words, if the buyer can make money off the option.

Options are labeled in terms of their company, expiration date and the exercise price that they specify. In other words, an Intel July 51 call option means that you have the option to purchase 100 shares of Intel stock for $51 per share before the option expires in July. A Microsoft May 110 put option means that you have the option to sell 100 shares of Microsoft stock for $110 per share before the May expiration date.

American vs. European-style Options

There are two different kinds of options – American-style and European-style. The most commonly traded options in the United States are American-style options. These options contracts can be exercised any time from the date of purchase until the date of expiration. In contrast, European-style options only allow you to exercise them at a special period of time before the expiration date.

Valuing Stock Options

There are three possibilities for labeling the value of a stock option: at the money, in the money, and out of the money. Both put and call options are considered to be at the money if the exercise price is equal to the current price of the stock. Put and call options are opposite, however, in terms of determining whether they are in or out of the money.

A put option is considered out of the money when its strike price is less than the current price of the underlying stock, and in the money when its strike price is greater than the current price of the stock. Conversely, a call option is out of the money when the strike price is greater than the stock's market price, and in the money when the strike price is less than the stock's current price.

There are two measurements of value that apply to stock options that are traded on the market – intrinsic value and time value. A stock option can only have intrinsic value if it is in the money. This value equals the difference between its strike price and the current price of the stock upon which it is based. The more in the money an option is, the more intrinsic value it will have. Time value, on the other hand, is dependent on the time that is left before an option expires; the more time there is, the greater chance there is that the stock will go up in value.

Taxes

Unlike employer-granted stock options, which are discussed in detail in the early chapters of this book, options contracts that you buy and sell, profits or losses from the stocks that you receive from exercising these contracts, and profits or losses that you have from buying or selling contracts themselves are all subject to capital gains taxes, not compensation income taxes. These are not providing you with compensation income, since they are investments in which you are participating on your own, with no connection to an employer.

The basic tax rules concerning options contracts revolve around short- and long-term capital gains – with tax liability determined according to how long you hold the contract, when or whether you exercise the contract, when or whether you buy or sell the underlying stock that you receive as the result of an exercise, and when or whether you sell the contract itself.

The main thing to remember is that if you engage in options trading, you will be subject to tax rules concerning capital gains and capital losses – which are profits and losses from capital investments – and some of these rules are similar to those which apply to regular stock investing. The tax rules concerning options trading, however, are complicated and multi-faceted, and it's best to consult with a tax advisor and the IRS to determine your tax liability as you figure your taxes for these investments. As you do with all of your investments, make sure to keep detailed records of all the put and call options you buy and sell, prices, profits, and losses. For more information about taxes and options trading, take a look at "Taxes and Investing: A Guide for the Individual Investor," a publication of the Chicago Board Options Exchange that is listed in the "Resources for Further Research" section later in this book.

Options Strategy

Options can provide you with a valuable means to protect yourself from some of the risks of the stock market. They are not infallible, but when used properly they can be a form of insurance against the potential downside of stock investing. The first thing to remember with options trading is that you don't want to put as much money into it as you do into your regular stock investing. This would make them far too risky for most people. Rather, you'll want to put a relatively small amount of money into options; when used this way, they can actually help reduce your overall risk. Options trading also requires somewhat more time and attention than investing in regular stocks; you'll have to keep an eye on your options and the market every day to make sure that you stay on top of prices and earnings potential.

The great thing about strategizing with stock options is that you can use them to match your own view of where the market is going. Whether you're bullish (thinking the market is heading up), bearish (thinking the market is heading down), or neutral (thinking the market is going to stay about the same), you can buy stock options that can benefit from any potential market scenario.

To formulate your options strategy, therefore, you first must have some idea of where the market is going. You'll also want to study particular stocks to figure out whether or not they will be following the general trend of the market or their sector. You can do all of this by reading business and investing publications, watching the news, and studying the annual reports and other information from particular companies. Most brokerages (both of the bricks-and-mortar and the online variety) offer an opportunity to research companies and the market as a whole. Just as you would for investing in individual stocks, you'll want to make full use of this research.

If after your research you think that the market is heading up, then you might decide to start investing in a small number of call options on selected stocks. You can purchase a call option with what you think is a favorable stock price, and then if the stock price does indeed go up, you'll have two paths of action before the expiration date. Either you can exercise the option and buy the underlying stock, or you can sell the option contract. In both cases, you could make a profit. If, however, the stock price falls, you might want to sell the contract to regain at least part of the premium that you paid; otherwise, when the expiration date rolls around your option contract will be worthless.

For those who think the market is heading down, put options can be a good choice. Essentially, you are buying the right to sell a stock at a fixed strike price. The more the stock price goes down, the more money you stand to make through the sale. As you can with a call contract, you can also sell the option contract itself. If the stock price goes up, however, you will lose the premium that you paid for the contract – but you won't stand to lose more than that. In this way, put options can minimize the downside risk, while letting you take full advantage of the upside potential for making money off a falling stock price.

A strategy for a more neutral market (or one that you think is more neutral) will involve careful attention to particular stocks themselves, instead of relying on a general view of market trends. In other words, in a neutral market some stocks will go up, and some will go down, and there will be various trends according to different sectors and industries. You'll want to study these stocks, sectors, and industries to come up with a particular strategy. In this case, your options portfolio might include a mix of puts and calls.

Since conventional stock options typically expire in nine months, they are more appropriate for a short-term strategy. If you want to strategize for the long-term – up to three years – you might want to try LEAPS. They can let you participate in the options market over a longer period of time, and they can also help you to guard against losses that you might otherwise experience.

This gives you a general introduction to the fascinating and fast-moving world of options trading. Strategizing with options, however, is not a simple matter; for more information, talk with your broker about what might work best in your individual situation.

Core Area 4

Interviews With Industry Visionaries

Christopher J. Loiacono, C.P.A.
Richard A. Eisner & Company
New York, New York

Christopher J. Loiacono, C.P.A. is a tax partner and co-chair of Richard A. Eisner & Company, LLP's New Media/Internet Group. He has experience working with publicly and privately held clients, including family groups and high net-worth individuals. Mr. Loiacono provides tax planning for companies and senior management in a number of industries, including new media, software developers, LBO investment advisors, manufacturing, wholesale distributors, and service businesses. Mr. Loiacono received his B.S. from the City University of New York and has been employed by Richard A. Eisner & Company for ten years.

Vivian Wagner: Have you seen an increase or decrease in stock options being given as part of employee benefits packages over the past several years?

Christopher Loiacono: Oh, absolutely an increase, and particularly in the technology sector – software and technology companies have obviously brought stock options to the forefront. Now, laypeople who never knew what a stock option was are getting stock options, and that was not done in the past. It's certainly increased dramatically. It has also affected other sectors, because in order to stay competitive and retain talent companies that are not even in the technology sector have had to think about equity plans.

VW: Have you noticed any kind of decrease at all in the last six or eight months since the stock market went down last spring? Have companies been offering them less, or are employees less willing to take them as part of a compensation package?

CL: I don't think they're being offered less, but they're no longer viewed as a trade-off for traditional compensation. Prior to the market correction, they were often viewed as a trade-off to the compensation package. If someone had a market value of $100,000, and you're a high-flying dotcom, you might be able to get that person for $75,000 cash and a significant options grant, because the options were viewed as having such a big upside. What I seeing happening is that tradeoff – that spread – has narrowed, but it has not gone away. People who are worth $100,000 now want $100,000, but they want the stock options too.

VW: What are some of the biggest advantages of stock options from the employer's perspective?

CL: It's a way of tying employees into the company's overall performance, and binding the employee for some period of time. Because the option is only worth something if there's an increase in the value of the underlying stock, it's a way of really getting that employee to not only think of his/her individual activities, but to think globally about the company. In addition, when you attach the vesting schedule and some other provisions, you're really asking that employee to stick around for a period of time so that those stock options vest.

VW: And from the employee's point of view, what would you say some of the biggest advantages are?

CL: Well, obviously there's the chance of a big windfall. Most wage earners have to look forward to next year's wage in order to realize some benefit. This way, there's a chance, at least, of a line employee achieving significant wealth by working for a dotcom or some other type of technology company.

VW: Are there disadvantages, from either the employer's or the employee's perspective?

CL: From the employee's perspective, due to the tax implications associated with stock options, the contractual limitations might mean that the employee is not getting what he or she thinks they are. Or, you may have to sell a significant portion of the stock you get from the exercise in order to pay for the taxes associated with the option. There could be contractual limitations that prohibit your ability to sell the options or to sell the stock. The company may be a private company, and there may not even be a market in which to sell the stock. So there are a number of gambles, particularly if you're working for a private company. One thing to consider is whether the company will go public – that's a big gamble. Or will it be acquired by a public company, that's another way to potentially get some liquidity.

Second, what contractual limitations – also referred to as a lock up, and there are some SEC restrictions as well – will prohibit me from selling the stock when I want to? There could be additional market risk. I mean, technology companies come out at very high IPO prices, and those prices tend to drop dramatically within the first year. If you're contractually locked up – prohibited from selling that stock – by the time your provisions expire, the stock price might have dropped dramatically. Let's say that your strike price is $1, and the company does an IPO at $15: That's terrific, but you might not be able to sell your stock when it's at $15 because of a lockup agreement with the underwriter. This is an SEC restriction, which means you may have to wait six months or a year in order to sell your stock. By this time it might have gone done to $2 or $3, and you're stuck. You have to bear the market risk and wait it out. In addition to that, you could face some really negative tax implications depending on when you exercised your options, and what the prices were when you exercised.

VW: What are some of the mistakes that people make in terms of taxes when they receive stock options from their employers?

CL: Mistake number one is not seeking out tax help from a qualified advisor.

VW: And a lot of people fail to do that?

CL: Yes. Second, they often make the mistake of relying on the advice of internal or in-house people, even colleagues, and sometimes the financial professionals in house. I find that in the private company sector, there can be significant turnover in the financial area and they may not get quality advice from the people in house. They're certainly not going to get quality advice from their fellow employees. So I think it's important to make an investment and seek out the advice of a professional upfront. And we'll talk about some of the major mistakes that can be made.

VW: How should they go about finding a professional? Would you recommend an accountant?

CL: I would recommend either a C.P.A. who specializes in taxation and has worked with executives that have stock options in their portfolio, or a tax attorney who has similar experience. They should seek these out through the normal channels – referrals from friends, and business affiliates.

VW: What fine print should employees make sure they understand when they receive a stock options agreement? In other words, what should they look for, what kinds of things should they understand in that agreement?

CL: Well, the first thing to do is to determine whether they received an ISO or a nonqualified, and that's generally right on the face of the option agreement. They should be looking at the terms of the vesting. Vesting can range anywhere from one to five years; it can vest monthly, quarterly, semi-annually or annually; it can vest pro-rata or it can vest based on the achievement of performance goals. There can be floors or trenches. It doesn't have to be pro-rata, it can be that a significant portion vests at the end of year one, and then the balance vests pro-rata over a two or three year period. There are really an unlimited number of permutations in terms of vesting. Now it's being said that companies don't want to track an unlimited number of vesting schedules; they want to keep it simple. Companies generally derive more of a boilerplate plan for the line employees, and they leave the true negotiations for when they are dealing with the core group of executives. They don't want to negotiate with middle managers and below. Those items are only negotiable at a certain level.

VW: Are there other things they should look for in the fine print?

CL: Yes. The biggest misnomer I've seen is in terms of the actual number of options they've received relative to the number of shares and options in the universe of that company. For example, if you receive a grant of 10,000 options at a private company, what does that really mean? How many shares are outstanding, and how many other options are outstanding as well? Particularly if you're one of the key management people, you should think in terms of a percentage of the company, and assess based on the raw number of options. For example, if you receive 10,000 options, but there are 100 million shares outstanding, then that has a certain meaning. If you receive 10,000 options and there are 1 million shares outstanding, then obviously that is significantly better.

VW: And how do you determine how many shares are outstanding?

CL: Ask. Of course, that advice is aimed at management people. Obviously, for the line employees, it's a little different. But for an early-stage private company where you're a COO or CTO, you should probably think of your rewards in terms of a percentage of the company. People should really ask, and be entitled to know, what the universe is.

VW: Is there also a stock option plan, typically, and do employees usually see that?

CL: There's usually a plan, and depending on the company, they may distribute a copy of the plan. Usually for the line employees they'll only distribute the agreement and then refer to the plan. The plan is a document that is approved generally by the board and the shareholders, and usually there's a concurrent authorization of shares. In other words, this plan has the ability to grant x number of options on y number of shares – and generally it's the same number. You can either have two plans – one for nonqualifieds and one for ISOs – or you can simply have one plan that covers both, and I generally see one plan that covers both types of options. The plan will also authorize a particular body within the firm to grant these awards, and may even list some of the criteria that this body can use. They usually try to keep it very general, though, so the body has some flexibility about how they grant them. They also determine the term of the plan and the term of the options.

VW: Now what are the differences in tax consequences between receiving a stock option and receiving shares of a stock outright?

CL: OK, good question. As we talked about with stock options, the taxable event is deferred until there is some type of event like an exercise. So the employee has the ability to control the timing of that event. When you grant shares outright, with no restrictions on them, the shares are taxable on the fair value of the shares immediately upon receipt. That's significant because the employee may have a liquidity problem in paying the taxes on that share award, and the employee may be forced to sell shares in order to pay the taxes. That's also significant because there may not be a market to sell those shares into, especially if it's a private company.

VW: How do stock options from public companies differ from those from private companies?

CL: The main difference is that there's a market for the shares, and their price is known. Two, for liquidity purposes, you have a better chance of being able to sell your shares into the marketplace. In the small cap area you might not be able to sell your shares, even though the company is public. But in a private company, figuring out the value of the shares is of course a very big issue.

Second, the market for those shares: does the company have to buy them back? Can the company buy them back? Are you prohibited from selling them to someone else? Generally that's probably true – there's probably a shareholder agreement that prohibits you from selling them. Usually the company has the right of first refusal. Those are all things to be considered. So let's go back to the question of receiving stock outright. What companies can also do is attach some vesting provisions with the shares received outright, so that similar to the options, there can be vesting provisions attached to these. This can actually exacerbate the tax problems as follows. If you receive shares subject to a substantial risk of forfeiture, which is really what vesting is – obviously if you leave the company before you vest, you forfeit the shares – then the taxable event is deferred until those restrictions begin to lapse. And when they lapse, you have taxable income at the fair value in place on the date of lapse. If the company is doing well, and the stock price increases, your taxable income increases accordingly.

So what can an employee do? There's something called an 83(b) election, which must be made within 30 days of receipt of the stock. What happens when you combine options and restricted stock? I have a very confusing set of circumstances. What we generally say is that the vesting provisions in this scenario are placed on the restricted stock, and the option itself is exercisable immediately. This is generally what you see in the marketplace. So they've moved the vesting provisions down to the stock, and they let the options be exercisable immediately. Obviously, vesting is attached to a timeline, so at any given point in time, you may have shares that are vested, and shares that are unvested. When you exercise your option with respect to the vested shares – the ones that you own now – you have some type of taxable event on the exercise. With respect to the unvested shares, you look at the typical restricted stock rules, and now you're looking at a taxable event being deferred into the future. So with respect to the unvested shares, you may now make your 83(b) election when you exercise the options.

VW: Is this happening fairly frequently now?

CL: I've seen it happen quite a bit in the dotcom area.

VW: Why is that?

CL: Well, what it's doing is adding some bells and whistles to the plan. It's giving the employees a few more options – no pun intended. If you just give employees stock options, and you have vesting provisions associated with that stock option, they have to wait for the vesting to lapse before they can exercise their stock options. By combining these two, you're giving the employees the ability to exercise earlier, and then make that 83(b) election with respect to the shares, should they choose to do that. You've given the employees the ability to accelerate things by combining these two together. You're not recommending that they do that, but you're giving them the ability to do that.

VW: Could we return to the question of how to determine the value of your stock options if you work for a private company?

CL: Well, it's a very difficult subject because the employee might not have all of the information available to him/her. Generally, management will have to let the employee know what the fair value is on that given day. There are a number of ways that management can determine what the value is. Obviously, the best way is to have some type of arms-length transaction so that there's a third-party transaction that management can point to and say, "Well, we just raised money – we just sold stock at a fundraising for x dollars per share, and we're pointing to that event as our benchmark." I would hope that event occurs at or near the time that the employee is exercising one of these stock transactions. That's the best of all worlds.

VW: And the worst of all worlds would be that no one has any idea?

CL: Well, the worst of all worlds is that the company assigns some value to it based on some factors that they take into consideration, which may not be the worst, but the weakest. Another way to do it is to have the company go out and hire a valuation firm to provide the valuation report, in other words to pay a third party to provide that information. Of course, the two bodies that are concerned about reviewing this information are the Internal Revenue Service and the SEC from the company's standpoint.

VW: In the end, which is preferable in terms of the taxes you would owe versus the money you stand to make—ISOs or NQSOs?

CL: It depends on timing. Obviously, with nonqualified options, all of the spread that exists (the income) will be subject to ordinary income tax rates, whereas with the ISO if you exercise and hold the stock, you can achieve long-term capital gain rates. However, that depends on when you exercise. And remember, you can minimize the taxes if you exercise when the fair value of the stock is relatively low, but you need two things. You need the cash to pay the exercise price, and you need the cash to pay any taxes generated on the exercise. If you do that – and exercise when the price is low – you can get the clock ticking for long-term capital gains, and then the future appreciation will all be subject to capital gains rates. But, once again you're limited to cash, and you're also obviously taking some risks. You're laying out cash today for the exercise price and the taxes, and you're hoping that the stock goes up. If it doesn't, then of course you have a loss. That's why it's really all about timing and cash flow.

VW: In regard to taxes, and maybe other issues, what's the best way of exercising?

CL: There are cashless exercises, and there's also something called pyramiding – which is a method of using existing shares to pay. Some option plans permit you to pay for the exercise price by using existing shares of the company stock.

VW: Which of those is preferable?

CL: There are no cookie cutter answers here, which is why I would recommend seeing an advisor. An advisor can lay out a sensitivity analysis, where you look at the fair value of the stock today versus what you think the fair value of the stock may be over periods of time. You also see what the difference is if you exercise today, in year one, or year two. The analysis will lay out all of these factors in a rational way so you can see what your alternatives are.

Pyramiding is pretty neat in that you can utilize the stock's full value for purposes of exercising options. Let's say for example that you have an option with an exercise price of $10, and you have 10 options, and you have one share of stock – and the fair value of the stock today is $100. You paid $1 for that share of stock, so you have $99 of appreciation with respect to that share of stock. You can use that one share of stock worth $100 to exercise those 10 options that each has an exercise price of $10. You would need $100 to exercise those 10 options, so you can use that one share of stock to exercise those 10 options without triggering that $99 gain on that single share of stock. That's pretty neat. However, you will have to live with whatever tax consequences there are on the ten options that you exercised. Remember, I just said the fair value was $100, and you exercised 10 options with an exercise price of $10; each of those options has $90 of spread, so whether they're ISOs or nonqualifieds determines what the tax consequences are going to be on those 10 options. But you still avoided picking up the $99 of gains on that one share of stock. This is great if you've been with a company for a while, and you have a mix of shares and options in your portfolio. It's a pretty neat thing if you can avail yourself of your existing shares.

VW: Can you think of anything we haven't covered?

CL: There are a couple of things we haven't talked about: the impact of lockups and loans and such items. Here's where people can really make big mistakes. When a company is doing an IPO, they enter into an agreement with the underwriter where management says that neither it nor the employees will sell their stock for a certain period of time after the date of the IPO. This is called a lock-up agreement. This is obviously to prevent employees from selling their stock into the market and bringing down the price, and it also looks pretty bad to the marketplace. The underwriter wants to support the stock price, so they enter into these lockup agreements, and they can be anywhere from three months to a year. Generally, they're about six months.

So, if at the time of an IPO an employee were to exercise his or her options and recognize that some type of taxable income event falls on that date, based on the fair value at that point in time, he or she would be prohibited from selling the underlying stock, so now there is a liquidity issue. And the company has a problem, too. These are nonqualified options, and the company has the requirement to withhold, and the employee has to fund this. Let's use some real world examples. Let's say that the employee has stock options with a strike price of $1. At the time of exercise, this stock has a fair value of $10, and these are nonqualified options. On the date of exercise, the employee recognizes $9 of taxable income. There's a withholding obligation, and taxes due on this $9. However, let's assume the employee is not wealthy, and he cannot come up with the taxes on that $9. In a normal scenario, the employee would probably sell the stock that he had just received, which is worth $10, to pay the taxes. Let's say, however, that the employee is subject to a lockup agreement, and he can't sell the stock. What happens? The company may lend him the money; he may borrow the money from some third party. However, the income event is fixed at that $9 of income. And now, the employee bears the risk of the market fluctuation until that lockup expires, before he can sell the stock and settle that loan obligation. And we all know what can happen: the stock can go down. But guess what: the liability does not go down. The liability is fixed.

VW: So the employee is kind of in a bind there.

CL: Got it.

VW: And what was the other thing you had mentioned?

CL: Sometimes brokerage houses or banks that are close to the company may offer loans to employees, or at least to key management people, so they can go out and exercise all of their options. They'll lend them the money to exercise the options and to pay the taxes. There's so much euphoria at a company that's going through an IPO; everyone believes that the stock is going to the moon. They get very caught up in it and don't look at the downside. I'll give you some case studies. Last year I advised three employees of a company that was about to go through an IPO. It was one of the high-profile IPOs in the dotcom area. One was a 25-year-old unmarried woman; one was a 35-year-old man with a mortgage and two children; one was a single woman in her late 30s. So, here were three very different risk profiles. There was so much momentum in the company to exercise their options, because it was thought that the stock price was going to go up very quickly. They really weren't focusing on the doomsday scenario. So when I laid out the pros and cons of exercising all of their options and borrowing the money to pay the taxes and the exercise price, and then described what would happen if the stock price went down, I received three very different reactions. The younger woman came from a fairly wealthy family, and was willing to borrow money from family members in order to take the risk. The 35-year-old man with a mortgage was not willing to take any risks, because he just couldn't afford the doomsday scenario. The woman in her late 30s who was single was kind of in the middle; she didn't exercise them all, but she exercised a small block of her options, and took some risk. She managed her risk. It was pretty much consistent with what I thought would happen. That's the thought process that goes into these scenarios.

INTERVIEWS WITH INDUSTRY VISIONARIES

Debra Brian
Director of Worldwide Compensation and Benefits
Intel Corporation
Santa Clara, California

Debra Brian is the Director of Worldwide Compensation and Benefits at Intel. She has been at Intel for about nine and a half years, and in human resources in the high tech industry since 1987. She is responsible for the research, design, implementation and marketing of compensation and benefits programs worldwide – including stock option plans, stock purchase plans, and medical, dental, and retirement plans. Ms. Brian has a B.A. in Psychology from University of Texas at Austin, and a M.S. in Management Science from the University of Texas at Dallas.

Vivian Wagner: What is the percentage of Intel employees who are offered stock options as part of their benefits package?

Debra Brian: It's 100 percent of all employees in countries that allow stock options. There are a couple of countries where we do a stock-in-lieu program – it's a bonus program, because you can't actually have a stock option program.

VW: Have 100 percent of all employees always received stock options?

DB: Actually, in 1997 we expanded our stock option program to include all employees – both exempt and non-exempt worldwide.

VW: So before that it was limited?

DB: It was restricted basically to the exempt population. And in 1997 we had a share-the-wealth kind of program. Actually, our employee bonus program is also a widespread program. All of our employees participate in it as well, rather than just the top executives. We're very inclusive.

VW: And what percentage of employees takes advantage of the stock option plan, or do they all automatically get them?

DB: They all automatically get them.

VW: What kinds of stock options does Intel offer?

DB: We grant nonqualified.

VW: Just nonqualified? You don't grant any incentive stock options?

DB: No.

VW: Why is that?

DB: We feel at this time that basically we have more flexibility with nonqualified stock options than we do with incentive stock options, and the Alternative Minimum Tax kind of decreases any benefit that you would receive from one.

VW: Has Intel been increasing or decreasing the total number of stock options that it has available for employees over the last couple of years?

DB: We've been granting more options. We have hired more employees; we're up to about 83,000 people.

VW: What are the biggest advantages that employees find in getting these stock options?

DB: What we really like about stock options is that it's an opportunity for our employees to share in the success of the company on a risk-free basis. Whereas a stockholder would have to pay money in order to buy a share of Intel stock, and in order to participate in any gains, our employees are granted stock options and they don't have to put any of their money on the table until they're ready to exercise. They can ride the gains up, and they can exercise and hold or exercise and sell. So it's a wonderful financial opportunity. It ties the interests of our employees directly with the stockholders. They're very keenly aware of how the stock is doing. I think it works very well for us. Another good thing is that if we do well financially, the employees do well.

VW: What kinds of advantages does Intel have from offering stock options?

DB: At Intel, we try to look at our total compensation package, our bonuses, our cash profit sharing, our deferred profit sharing, stock options, and this allows us to keep our fixed costs a little lower. Then we share through our variable programs, such as our employee bonus or our cash profit sharing, when we can afford to do so, and so employees see a larger package and we keep lower fixed costs.

VW: Have employees expressed any disadvantages, or are there disadvantages for Intel?

DB: We've been fortunate that we've been very successful financially, so our bonus programs have paid out well. Our profit-sharing contributions have been at 12.5 percent for the last 12 years, so employees have seen a bounty of financial rewards. They've shared in the success of the company. With that kind of track record, I don't see much of a downside. There is a risk assumed when you come in because we have more leverage – we have a lot of leverage in our program.

VW: Do you have vesting schedules? Are they the same for all employees?

DB: Our vesting schedule right now is as follows: When you're hired in at Intel, you're recommended for a stock option grant, and basically you vest 20 percent of that grant per year and after five years you're 100 percent vested. Following your hire into Intel, we have a review process, and that occurs in April. Then, based on your performance you receive an additional recommendation for stock options. And that vests five years from the time of grant. And what this does for us, it actually forces employees to hold the stock longer, and gives the stock time to appreciate.

VW: What is the typical number of shares that are offered? Do you have a set number of shares for managers, or secretaries?

DB: It varies from the lower level up to the higher level. People are a lot more leveraged at the higher level of the organization. A lot more of their income is through stock options, maybe significantly more than 50 percent. There are fewer stock options at lower levels of the organization. Part of that is due to market practice, and part of it is due to the fact that as you go higher in the organization, you have more impact on Intel and the direction that we set.

VW: What are some of the basic features of a stock option agreement you receive when you're hired at Intel? You've gone over the vesting schedule a little bit – are there other kinds of limitations?

DB: No, and we grant the stock options at fair market value.

VW: Do you offer stock options to non-employees or independent consultants?

DB: Only to the board of directors.

VW: Does Intel human resources department provide information or counseling to employees who have questions about their stock options?

DB: We provide written materials on the website. We have seminars on stock options that we offer to our employees. We also have an on-call assistance center, which consists of a telephone bank of employees who are available to answer individual employee questions or managerial questions about any of our compensation and benefit programs or Human Resources policy. They can call us and ask questions. Also, they're allowed to call our supplier to get their questions answered as well.

VW: What kind of help does Intel offer to employees who are ready to exercise their options? Do you help them through that process?

DB: Basically, they can exercise their options through a voice response system, a telephone system. They can do it with a participant service representative, so they can talk to a real-live service person and exercise it. And our international sites also have the option of a fax method, so they can be walked through the entire process with a live person if that's what they'd like, or they can do something a little more automated if they're comfortable with the process.

VW: And what sorts of choices do they have for exercising? Do you offer a cashless exercise choice?

DB: Yes we do.

VW: Do you provide loans for exercising?

DB: No we don't – no loans.

VW: Is it true that employees do have a choice as to whether or not to receive stock options as a part of their compensation package?

DB: Well, they receive stock options automatically. Whether they choose to exercise them or not is their choice.

VW: Does Intel consider stock options as a perk that is added on to regular income, or do the options actually replace a part of the income?

DB: We actually feel it's part of the total compensation package, so we do look at the totality beyond just the paycheck. We do a personal portrait compensation and benefits statement on an annual basis for our employees to let them know about all of the compensation and benefits programs, and to give them an idea of what they're really making. In addition to stock options, we have a cash profit-sharing program, we have an employee bonus program, we have a deferred profit-sharing program, and then we have various benefits that we offer to our employees. So we try to show them what the value of their total package is worth. We see it as an integral part of our total package.

VW: With the recent market downturn, and the value of Intel stock dropping, have stock options become less popular with Intel employees? Are they expressing concern?

DB: I think they're just as popular. I think you'll find that all high tech workers are a little bit concerned about the market right now, and a lot of investors are concerned about the market. We see it as a short-term issue. We fully expect that we'll continue to perform, and the market will reward us, and there will be a turnaround. There is some concern about it, but I think that's perfectly natural.

VW: What future trends do you see in regard to employee stock options, both at Intel and elsewhere?

DB: I think that more and more companies will offer stock options. I think they're an excellent vehicle to engage employees in trying to make the company financially successful. I think they understand very quickly the relationship between how the market views our success and what happens with stock prices. Our employees have enjoyed that, and I think that you will see more and more companies use stock options as part of their package. I think it's also a good thing for the stock holders, because then the employees have basically the same interest that they have and they want to make things work. It's really important for them, too.

Core Area 5

Excerpts From Experienced Individuals

Mark I. Gruhin
Schmeltzer, Aptaker & Shepard, P.C.
Partner

The Ups and Downs of Stock Options

There is often a lot of confusion about incentive stock options, non-statutory incentive stock options, restricted stock agreements and the tax implications of these and other choices. It seems that everyone wants to offer ISOs, not necessarily because they're best for the business – since it depends on the type of business that one is in – but because these are tools needed to attract good employees, whether or not there might be other alternatives. From a tax perspective, there is a distinction between ISOs and nonqualified options. However, little emphasis has been placed on the Alternative Minimum Tax implications to employees so they really don't understand that ISOs aren't necessarily as good as they might seem.

In terms of capitalization and the employment arena, you often see distinctions between preferred stock and common stock according to a valuation. This is done primarily to recognize the difference between how a company requires a financier to evaluate a company versus how a company needs to value itself in order to attract employees of quality. Ultimately, those two valuations need to merge. Sometimes problems occur when valuations are too high and market changes create "down rounds." These events can accelerate the loss of a high-tech startup company's most valuable possession, its human resources. Other problems sometimes occur with regard to the chemistry between the representatives of the investors and the founders of a company. Expectations need to be clear from the beginning in order to avoid management meltdown.

Arnold Levine
Proskauer Rose, L.L.P.
Chair, iPractice Group

Tax Consequences of Stock Options

There's a major tax consideration involved in granting stock options below market value. Companies are under a lot of pressure to issue below market stock options to executives and to employees. The consequence of this is that these will incur ordinary income tax liabilities rather than tax-favored capital gains treatment for the holders. Also, this can trigger a tax at the time of exercise of the option rather than at the time of sale. Again, it's not a question of mistakes. It involves balancing the desire for a cheaper option price against the resulting adverse tax consequences.

Another thing that sometimes happens in this context is that there are some significant expense recognition items for accounting purposes that are generated by stock option plans. If the stock option plan has a below market price or has a feature that allows the option holder to use appreciation of the stock option to pay for shares of stock, the company might be required to revalue the stock option periodically and treat the enhancement in value as compensation to the employees and others receiving those stock options. The result is the company being required to recognize an expense item that can run into the multi-millions of dollars when the company reports its earnings.

EXCERPTS

Stock Option Misperceptions

There is a lack of sophistication about the tax consequences. People have to carefully think through and understand the tax consequences. Most executives aren't aware of the accounting implications and the charge to earnings that will flow from many of the stock options they're granted. Sometimes in the early stages a young company wants to do things very cheaply and they don't want to spend a lot of time with lawyers, or they're hiring lawyers who will work very cheaply and it won't be very sophisticated work. They will end up doing some things that will have later tax consequences to various parties and accelerated charges against earnings.

One other thing is very important. You have to be very sensitive in how you word the preemptive right protection granted to early-stage investors. Preemptive rights entail a grant to a shareholder of rights to purchase additional shares in the event of future sales. If these provisions are not drafted carefully, it can be burdensome later on. I've seen situations where it's drafted poorly and the early money gets a chance to refrain from investing in the second, third and fourth rounds and when the fifth round comes up they have the opportunity to recapture the same original percentage of the company that they owned, even though they didn't participate in rounds two, three or four. If one is not careful that can give rise to some significant problems.

In the early stages of raising money one must also be very careful to think through all of the securities laws implications. If you do some careless private placements where you are not careful about securities laws compliance in the early rounds of financing, then when you have a major opportunity to either raise money or do a merger, you may find your new investor or merger partner unhappy. They don't want to be subject to significant liabilities under the securities laws. There are private placements rules, called

Reg D, which allow you to sell to a large number of accredited investors, i.e., people who have a million dollar net worth or income of $200,000 for several years. If all your investors are accredited, then you don't have to give them any special form of disclosure, even financial information disclosure, although you must avoid being misleading in what you do give them. Once you bring in some investors who are not accredited – and often that's the case with friends and family – then you're in a situation where unless you give them very detailed disclosure (equivalent to disclosure contained in a public offering, in certain cases even ensuring that they're represented by a "purchaser representative") then those offers are subject to other exposures under the securities laws.

If somewhere down the line you are doing a transaction involving a merger into another company, for which the acquiring company is issuing the stock in exchange for your shares, the buyer may be afraid to do the deal because of potential securities law exposure. I was in a situation where the company was being sold to a very promising technology company that was about to go public. The buyer, which was going public, was very sensitive about having any issues in their registration statement arising from the failure of the acquired company to comply with the securities laws. The buyer was also concerned about the fact that the acquirer would be issuing its shares to people who were not "accredited investors." We ultimately solved the problem, but it almost killed the deal.

The main lesson here is to be careful in every aspect of your fundraising. Even if the amounts are small, comply with the federal and state securities laws and go to the trouble of doing it right. It is a pain in the neck and it is costly when you have non-accredited investors. It may be best to avoid being a nice guy and not allow your cousin and your friend in the deal if they're not accredited investors, because later on you may come to regret it.

EXCERPTS

James Hutchinson
Hogan & Hartson L.L.P
Partner

Understanding Stock Options

What is amazing to me is how little the average person understands about what they're getting. There are surveys that show the great majority of all options exercised result in ordinary income treatment to the holder, which is completely counter to the goal of incentive stock option plans and the relief provided under tax laws. If used right, incentive plans allow employees to get paid with equity, defer immediate taxes and then ultimately receive capital gains treatment. You're talking about the difference between a 20 percent tax and an almost 40 percent tax. It can be a fairly substantial amount. It's just interesting when everybody's pulling for that golden option ring but they're not really cognizant of what it means.

Vesting Trends

In the mid-Atlantic region literally nine times out of ten you will see a four-year vest, with 25 percent of the stock vesting at the end of the first year (a cliff vesting) and then monthly thereafter. Almost every deal is like that, which to me is sort of funny. If I'm in a tight labor market and I want to attract good people, and people care so much about the options, being aggressive with options would be an easy way to distinguish yourself. It's remarkable how infrequently it happens.

However, Silicon Valley seems to lead developments on these issues. One of our biggest clients just went into business a couple of months ago. They got $200 million of financing in April, and they filed to go public on the last day of September. They were billed as the largest first round VC financing ever at $200 million.

Typically options vest over time. We represented the management team, and they have structured their incentive stock options for their core first-round employees so that they "reverse vest." Employees get immediately vested options that are then subject to repurchase by the Company. They were granted an option the day they started, it was immediately vested, and the company lent them money to exercise. The beauty of this approach is that the holding period to ensure capital gains treatment starts sooner than it would with a traditional option grant.

Tim Bixby
LivePerson
CFO

What to Look for in an Internet Company

I think it's more important than ever to understand what the company does, what they're selling, and that it's a real product. You should even be able to get an idea about highly technical products. Akamai is a good example of this: it's essentially a bunch of clever Ph.D.s, and they've come up with a great technology, but their concept is "we make the Web work faster." Everybody gets that. It makes complete sense. So even on the technical side you can evaluate the value that these companies are bringing pretty easily. There are a lot of other companies that have a really cool idea, but if it doesn't satisfy a consumer need, if it's not something people want to do, then just because it's great technology doesn't mean it's going to be a great concept.

You've got to look at your worst-case scenario. Think about how bad that is. For a while there was a little bit too much riding on the fact that the stock options had to explode into huge, quick cash value. I think that pretty soon you'll see numbers on what the actual success rates are in terms of how many people moved from traditional businesses to startup businesses, and what the average benefit has been. It's going to be, with some pretty small exceptions, a lot like any other growing industry. Yes, there's a big shift, but a year into it or three years into it people are going to be doing the same things they were doing before. They'll be looking for interesting jobs or places where they'll be well paid, and where they're excited to come to work.

David R. Henkel
Agillion.com
CFO

Internet Companies and Stock Options

Stock options have helped Internet companies to attract and retain the employees that they need to be successful. Using stock options for this purpose is increasingly popular across many industries. However, the effect and the benefit is the most pronounced in industries where growth opportunities are rapid, such as the Internet. To convince a person with excellent career prospects in a particular industry to change industries and take on the career risk of changing industries, it takes an appropriate reward. Stock options can be that reward.

The current rapid pace of change in the Internet space has allowed some companies to rapidly establish a dominant position in a sector. This has led to unusually rapid increases in capitalization and share value for some companies. For employees associated with these companies, the related benefits have been spectacular due to their option positions. In other industries such increases in share value have been achieved, but the timeframes have been much longer. Also, stock options have not usually played such a significant role in the overall compensation packages of employees in other industries. The reward prospects from stock options have been successful in attracting large numbers of highly talented employees from other industries. This talent pool in turn has been successful in driving the entire Internet industry to grow and achieve success beyond most people's expectations.

Public vs. Private Companies

The technical framework exists to value stock options for both public and private companies. The difficulty usually lies in the lack of operating history for private companies. As an employee, the task is often equally difficult for both public and private companies, since the real question is how well a company will succeed. For a private company, the additional uncertainty is whether or not the company will ever have an opportunity to become public or be acquired in a way that the options will have value.

To sort this out, an employee needs to focus on what factors are the most important to his or her individual situation. Timeframe is the first issue. Stock options often have a 10-year life, but much of the uncertainty will be resolved in the first 2 or 3 years. Option vesting also generally ranges from 3 to 5 years, so it is important to take this factor into account. Pick a timeframe that is reasonable for you to stay at the company if it is moderately successful. Employers use the vesting period to incentivize employees to stay at least that long, but employees tend to look for new opportunities before that period has elapsed. Of course, if the company is wildly successful, you will have "golden handcuffs" that may effectively prevent you from leaving. There are worse problems to have.

After you have considered the timeframe, consider the reasonable price appreciation that could occur in your stock. Check how competitors have done, consider trends in the industry, and see if management will impart any of their thinking on the subject.

Here private companies often have an advantage. The pre-IPO value of a company's stock is often significantly lower than the post IPO price. This reflects the considerable uncertainty that most companies face in being able to deliver on their plans to go public. With a pre-IPO option valuation, the reasonable price appreciation may be significant if the company is successful in going public. An additional benefit of pre-IPO options is that they are usually much easier to exercise and hold (due to lower prices). Assuming that the options are ISO's, exercising and holding such shares for the mandated time period can significantly reduce the taxes on the ultimate sale. This can be a huge factor for options with a very small amount of cash necessary to exercise and hold.

The ultimate question is how high the stock can reasonably be expected to go given industry and other factors during the applicable timeframe. This is the same issue that the investor faces. Accordingly, the same factors govern: the capability of management, the competitive landscape, and the overall opportunity in the space.

What Employees Need to Understand about Finance

It is difficult to generalize what every employee must understand. Employees with good functional skills that are in demand by many different types of industries (LAN engineers, for example), may not need to understand much about the finances of the business or even the industry. If one company doesn't work out, they can always get a job elsewhere. With the current low level of unemployment, it seems like more people are adopting this attitude. However, for employees who are giving up significant cash compensation for the prospect of future income from bonuses or stock options, then it is more important than ever that they understand the basics of the company's business plan. If the business plan involves cash expenses that exceed cash income for an extended period of time, then a more careful understanding of the business model needs to be undertaken.

Nothing supports job security like cash. Employers that are short of cash often use what they have to keep employees at the expense of all other possible uses. Cash that is on hand, can be borrowed or can be raised (in that order) is important for employees to understand. Certainly it helps if a business is already generating cash from operations. However, if employees focus only on such companies they will be missing out on many good opportunities. Once again, the quality and experience of management in raising and effectively managing the use of cash should be a prime concern to employees.

Negotiating a Fair Compensation Package

When it comes to compensation for individual employees, both parties need to have some degree of flexibility. The basic tradeoff that an early-stage Internet company faces is how to attract the best key employees with the least cash and stock options. Employees coming from large companies can expect to have the entire "bonus" portion of their compensation replaced by stock-related compensation and the promise of a cash bonus in the future when the company is on more solid financial ground. This may be acceptable to many people, but the difficulty is usually the toughest when the Internet company also proposes a reduced salary and limits up front moving and other costs. Cash is at such a premium in the early stage of a company that any cash expenditure that can be avoided can be translated into a higher valuation on the next round of a staged funding.

The possibility of very large rewards from future stock appreciation is the major financial "carrot" that Internet companies can hold out to employees. The value of this reward is difficult to determine, and, accordingly, most employees end up requiring a basic level of compensation on which they can live. What employees sometimes fail to take into account is that other income from a working spouse or investment returns from previous jobs may be sufficient to support a compensation structure that has a reduced salary and greater options. This is especially true of older employees who become risk averse. If employees would stand back and assess their entire financial picture, they would probably find that the lower level of salaries paid by Internet startup companies are easier to accept.

One option to consider is to request that the base salary be moved up to a level that is closer to the market level if the company is successful in raising additional funding. In this way, employees can limit the amount of stock that they need to sell in order to cover living expenses.

Joan Platt
CBS MarketWatch
CFO

Stock Options as Recruiting Tool: Then and Now

I've been here for 20 years and stock options have always been key. Actually the difference is because the unemployment rate is so low. It used to be that you'd have a startup and you'd offer options, and you could offer a lower salary. Today that's not true. You're offering the salary, bonus, and then the stock options on top of it.

It used to be a tool. Today, you've got to match everyone out there.

It's interesting, I found it a better tool 10 to 20 years ago than it is today. Today it's a given. Before, you could use it; now, people expect it, they almost think of it as a guarantee.

EXCERPTS

Public vs. Private Companies

If a company is privately held, you should get more shares. The risk is higher that it will never pop. For a while it didn't seem like there was any risk, as so many companies were going public. Now it's back as the market's much tighter. When you're in a public company, you actually get less stock, but you are in an established public company, which should mean less risk. The key is to determine how successful the company will be in the long term and how interested the public investment community is in the company's market.

Mary Dridi
WebMethods
CFO

The Benefits of Stock Options

I think stock options are an excellent recruiting tool and an excellent thing for companies in general. If you put the proper emphasis on them, and make people understand not only what options are worth to them but how they can really impact the value of those options, they can be a great tool.

We like the fact that all employees are owners. We want to really give them the sense of responsibility and ownership and how they can affect that not only for themselves but for other shareholders. I think that's very important. I don't think options will go away. It's possible they will become an even more meaningful part of compensation plans; we see people becoming more and more appreciative of options.

However, the one thing I have noticed is that candidates have difficulties comparing options offered by two or more companies. I've had many, many conversations where people say, but Company X offered me 10,000 and you're only offering me

5,000—and all they are looking at is the absolute number of shares. Then I would ask a couple of simple questions. How many shares do they have outstanding? What are their revenues? How do you compare their potential opportunity to ours? Who is backing the company? And they will respond that they don't know. I would try to explain that it's like comparing how many yen you're going to get versus how many dollars and only looking at the absolute number and not the underlying value. You can't do that type of comparison.

The other thing I would say more to employers as well as to potential employees is that you never want to have to do a reverse stock split on employees. Although the real value has not changed, perceptually it's a very negative thing in the employees' minds. Employees who were given a huge amount of options later find out that it was just because the base of the shares was so large. So they thought they were getting a lot more than they were – especially if they only looked at the number of options without regards to the number of shares outstanding.

So you've got to be very careful. Employees don't need to go through a lot of mathematical calculations, but when they are comparing one company's option grant to another they may want to look at the number of shares outstanding and take that into consideration, especially when the size of the option grants are significantly different. You also may want to take into consideration what funding stage the company's in. If it's an earlier stage company, they're most likely going to do many more rounds of financing versus one that may be very close to an IPO; at the same time, the number of shares being offered will be higher and the exercise price will be lower in an earlier stage company.

Having said all that, I think it really comes down more to which company and management team you believe in and which one you think has the greater potential. So while you can take certain of my above comments into consideration, the real decision should be based on your confidence and belief in the company and the management team.

What to Look for Regarding a Company's Finances

I'm not sure I would expect people to really get into a lot of the details of the financials. Certainly if the company will provide that, that would be information that would be nice to see. I think asking the profitability question, and asking when and if the company plans to go public can be beneficial. Again, most of those answers will be a little bit vague for obvious reasons. It's probably more important to look at who the financial backers are, what kind of companies they have backed, how much money has been invested to date and how much the company actually has in the bank today. It is also important to get an understanding of the market opportunity the company addresses.

It would be interesting to know what the revenues are, assuming the company is producing revenues. I'm just not sure how much a private company's going to tell you before you become an employee. If you aren't able to get detailed financial information you should look at the number and quality of customers and how the customer base has increased. It's going to be even harder to get information on projections, but if they will give you an idea of when they expect to reach profitability, that would be helpful to know.

But I think you're not going to get a lot of that detailed financial information from private companies. What's important is looking at the backers, and just talking to the employees. The confidence of the employee base, getting an understanding of who the management team is and how comfortable and confident you are with that management team can give you a good idea about the company.

My decision to join webMethods at a very early stage was based on three things: my confidence in management's ability to execute, my belief in the market opportunity and the fact that a well respected firm, FBR Technology Venture partners, had backed the company.

Core Area 6

Case Studies & Worksheets

I. Case Study

Just in case you've been curious about what a stock option plan looks like, here is an example, courtesy of Intel Corporation. You'll want to ask your company for a copy of your own stock option plan and agreement, and it's always a good idea read the fine print.

INTEL CORPORATION

1997 STOCK OPTION PLAN

(Amended and Restated Effective July 16, 1997)

1. PURPOSE

The purpose of this Intel Corporation 1997 Stock Option Plan (the "Plan") is to advance the interests of Intel Corporation, a Delaware corporation (hereinafter "Intel"), by stimulating the efforts of non-officer employees who are selected to be participants by heightening the desire of such persons to continue in working toward and contributing to the success of Intel. Stock options granted pursuant to this Plan are not incentive stock options, as defined in Section 422 of the Internal Revenue Code of 1986, as amended (the "Code").

2. DEFINITIONS

(a.) "Board of Directors" means the Board of Directors of Intel.

(b.) "Committee" means the Board of Directors and/or a committee of the Board of Directors acting pursuant to its authorization to administer this Plan under Section 4.

(c.) "Common Stock" means Intel Corporation's Common Stock, par value $.001, as presently constituted, subject to adjustment, and including other securities, as provided in Section 8.

(d.) "Corporation" means Intel and its Subsidiaries and affiliates, unless the context otherwise requires.

(e.) "Plan" means the Intel Corporation 1997 Stock Option Plan.

(f.) "Subsidiary" means any corporation (other than Intel) in an unbroken chain of corporations beginning with Intel where each of the corporations in the unbroken chain other than the last corporation owns stock possessing 50 percent or more of the total combined voting power of all classes of stock in one of the other corporations in such chain.

(g.) "Immediate Family" means the spouse, children and grandchildren of the Participant (as defined in Section 5 hereof).

3. COMMON STOCK SUBJECT TO THE PLAN AND TO OPTIONS

Subject to adjustment as provided in Section 8, the maximum number of shares of Common Stock which may be issued pursuant to this Plan shall not exceed 130,000,000 shares (as adjusted automatically by the Plan's terms effective July 13, 1997, to reflect a stock split effected in the form of a stock distribution). Shares issued under this Plan may be authorized and unissued shares of Common Stock or shares of Common Stock reacquired by Intel. All or any shares of Common Stock subject to an option which for any reason are not issued under an option may again be made subject to an option under the Plan.

4. ADMINISTRATION OF THE PLAN

The Plan shall be administered by the Board of Directors and/or by a Committee of the Board of Directors of Intel, as appointed from time to time by the Board of Directors. The Board of Directors shall fill vacancies on and from time to time may remove or add members to the Committee. Notwithstanding the foregoing, unless otherwise restricted by the Board of Directors, the Committee may appoint one or more separate committees (any such committee, a "Subcommittee") composed of one or more directors of Intel (who may but need not be members of the Committee) and may delegate to any such Subcommittee(s) the authority to grant options under the Plan to Participants (as defined in Section 5 hereof), to determine all terms of such options, and/or to administer the Plan or any aspect of it. Any action by any such Subcommittee within the scope of such delegation shall be deemed for all purposes to have been taken by the Committee. The Committee shall act pursuant to a majority vote or majority written consent.

Subject to the express provisions of this Plan, the Committee shall be authorized and empowered to do all things necessary or desirable in connection with the administration of this Plan, including, without limitation: (a) to prescribe, amend and rescind rules and regulations relating to this Plan and to define terms not otherwise defined herein;

(b) to determine which persons are Participants, to which of such Participants, if any, an option shall be granted hereunder and the timing of any such option grants; (c) to determine the number of shares of Common Stock subject to an option and the exercise or purchase price of such shares; (d) to establish and verify the extent of satisfaction of any conditions to exercisability applicable to an option, (e) to waive conditions to and/or accelerate exercisability of an option, either automatically upon the occurrence of specified events (including in connection with a change of control of the Corporation) or otherwise in its discretion; (f) to prescribe and amend the terms of option grants made under this Plan (which need not be identical); (g) to determine whether, and the extent to which, adjustments are required pursuant to Section 8 hereof; and (h) to interpret and construe this Plan, any rules and regulations under the Plan and the terms and conditions of any option granted hereunder, and to make exceptions to any such provisions in good faith and for the benefit of the Corporation.

All decisions, determinations and interpretations by the Committee regarding the Plan, any rules and regulations under the Plan and the terms and conditions of any option granted hereunder, shall be final and binding on all Participants and optionholders. The Committee shall consider such factors as it deems relevant, in its sole and absolute discretion, to making such decisions, determinations and interpretations including, without limitation, the recommendations or advice of any officer or other employee of the Corporation and such attorneys, consultants and accountants as it may select.

5. PARTICIPANTS

Any person who is an employee of the Corporation (a "Participant") shall be eligible to be considered for the grant of an option hereunder unless such person is an "officer or director" as contemplated by Rule 4460 of the Nasdaq Stock Market's National Market rules. No option shall be granted to any Participant if immediately after the grant of such option such Participant would own stock, including stock subject to outstanding options previously granted to him or her, amounting to more than five percent (5%) of the total combined voting power or value of all classes of stock of Intel. Any person designated by the Corporation as an independent contractor shall not be treated as an employee under the Plan.

6. GRANT, TERMS AND CONDITIONS OF OPTIONS

Options may be granted at any time and from time to time prior to the termination of the Plan to Participants selected by the Committee. However, subject to adjustment pursuant to Section 8, the aggregate number of shares of Common Stock subject to options granted under this Plan during any calendar year to any one Participant shall not exceed one percent (1%) of the number of shares of Common Stock outstanding on December 28, 1996. No optionholder shall have any rights as a stockholder with respect to any shares of Common Stock subject to an option hereunder until said shares have been issued. Options granted pursuant to the Plan need not be identical but each option shall be subject to the following terms and conditions:

(a) Price: The exercise price for each option shall be established by the Committee. The exercise price shall not be less than the fair market value of the stock on the date of grant. The exercise price shall be paid in full at the time of exercise. The exercise price shall be paid in such form of consideration as the Committee in its discretion shall specify, which may but need not include, e.g., in cash, by loan (as described in Section 7), by payment under an arrangement with a broker where payment is made pursuant to an irrevocable direction to the broker to deliver all or part of the proceeds from the sale of the option shares to the Corporation, by the surrender of shares of Common Stock owned by the optionholder exercising the option or issuable under an option held by the optionholder and having a fair market value on the date of exercise equal to the option price, or by any combination of the foregoing.

(b) Duration and Exercise or Termination of Option: Each option shall be exercisable in such manner and at such times as the Committee shall determine. However, each option granted must expire within a period of not more than ten (10) years from the grant date. The effective date of each option granted hereunder shall be the date on which the grant was made.

(c) Suspension or Termination of Option: The Chief Executive Officer, President, Chief Operating Officer, Vice President for Human Resources and General Counsel of the Corporation (any such person, an "Authorized Officer") each may provide at any time (including after a notice of exercise has been delivered) and from time to time that the right to exercise an option may be suspended pending a determination by an Authorized Officer or the Committee on whether a Participant to whom the option was granted or an optionholder has committed an act of embezzlement, fraud, dishonesty, nonpayment of any obligation owed to the Corporation, breach of fiduciary duty or deliberate disregard of Corporation rules; has made an unauthorized disclosure of any Corporation trade secret or confidential information; has engaged in any conduct constituting unfair competition; has induced any customer of the Corporation to breach a contract with the Corporation or any principal for whom the Corporation acts as agent to terminate such agency relationship; or has engaged in any other act or conduct proscribed by the Committee from time to time (any such act or conduct, individually or collectively, sometime hereinafter referred to as "Misconduct"). No person shall be entitled to exercise any option granted to a Participant or held by an optionholder if the Authorized Officer or the Committee, as the case may be, has determined such Participant or optionholder to have engaged in any Misconduct.

(d) Conditions and Restrictions Upon Securities Subject to Options: The Committee may provide that the shares of Common Stock issued upon exercise of an option shall be subject to such further conditions or agreements as the Committee in its discretion may specify prior to the exercise of such option, including without limitation, conditions on vesting or transferability, forfeiture or repurchase provisions and method of payment for the shares issued upon exercise (including the actual or constructive surrender of Common Stock already owned by the Participant). The Committee may establish rules for the deferred delivery of Common Stock upon exercise of an option with the deferral evidenced by use of "Stock Units" equal in number to the number of shares of Common Stock whose delivery is so deferred. A "Stock Unit" is a bookkeeping entry representing an amount equivalent to the fair market value of one share of Common Stock. Stock Units represent an unfunded and unsecured obligation of the Corporation except as otherwise provided by the Committee. Settlement of Stock Units upon expiration of the deferral period shall be made in Common Stock or otherwise as determined by the Committee. The amount of Common Stock, or other settlement medium, to be so distributed may be increased by an interest factor or by dividend equivalents. Until a Stock Unit is so settled, the number of shares of Common Stock represented by a Stock Unit shall be subject to adjustment pursuant to Section 8. Any Stock Units that are settled after the holder's death shall be distributed to the holder's designated beneficiary(s) or, if none was designated, the holder's estate.

(e) Transferability of Option: Unless otherwise provided by the Committee and subject to the establishment of procedures by the Committee, each option shall be transferable only:

(1) by will or the laws of descent and distribution, or

(2) by gift to the Immediate Family, partnerships whose only partners are the Participant or members of the Immediate Family,

limited liability companies whose only shareholders are the Participant or members of the Immediate Family, and trusts established solely for the benefit of the Participant or members of the Immediate Family.

The transferees described in this subsection ((d)) of Section 0 shall be referred to as "Permitted Transferees".

Options are transferable only to the extent the options are exercisable at the time of transfer. Any purported assignment, transfer or encumbrance that does not qualify under subsections (1) and (2) above shall be void and unenforceable against the Corporation.

The terms of stock options granted pursuant to this Plan shall apply to the beneficiaries, executors and administrators of the Participant and to Permitted Transferees (including the beneficiaries, executors and administrators of Permitted Transferees), including the right to agree to any amendment of the applicable option agreement, except that options transferred to Permitted Transferees shall not be transferable except by will or the laws of descent and distribution.

(f) <u>Cancellation</u>: The Committee may, at any time prior to exercise and subject to consent of the Participant, cancel any option previously granted and may or may not substitute in its place an option at a different price and different type under different terms or in different amounts.

(g) <u>Other Terms and Conditions</u>: Options may also contain such other provisions, which shall not be inconsistent with any of the foregoing terms, as the Committee shall deem appropriate. No option, however, nor anything contained in the Plan shall confer upon any Participant any right to continue in the Corporation's employ or service nor limit in any way the Corporation's right to terminate his or her employment or service at any time. Option grants may be evidenced by a written agreement and/or such other written arrangements as may be approved from time to time by the Committee.

7. LOANS

The Corporation may, in the sole discretion of the Committee, make loans for the purpose of enabling the Participant to exercise an option granted under the Plan and to pay the tax liability resulting from an option exercise under the Plan. The Committee shall have full authority to determine the terms and conditions of such loans. Such loans may be secured by the shares of Common Stock received upon exercise of such option.

8. ADJUSTMENT OF AND CHANGES IN SECURITIES

(a) If the outstanding securities of the class(es) then subject to this Plan are increased, decreased or exchanged for or converted into cash, property or a different number or kind of shares or other securities, or if cash, property or shares or other securities are distributed in respect of such outstanding securities, in either case as a result of a reorganization, reclassification, dividend (other than a regular, quarterly cash dividend) or other distribution, stock split, reverse stock split, spin-off or the like, or if substantially all of the property and assets of the Corporation are sold, then, unless the terms of such transaction shall provide otherwise, the maximum number and type of shares or other securities that may be subject to options and issued in accord with this Plan shall be appropriately adjusted. The Committee shall determine in its sole discretion the appropriate adjustment to be effected pursuant to the immediately preceding sentence. In addition, in connection with any such change in the class(es) of securities then subject to this Plan, the Committee may make appropriate and proportionate adjustments in the number and type of shares or other securities or cash or other property that may be acquired pursuant to options theretofore granted under this Plan and the exercise price of such options, and including coordinate adjustments in the number of shares of Common Stock represented by Stock Units (as referred to in Section 6(d) hereof).

(b) In the event that, otherwise than as provided in subsection (a) above, there shall be a change in the number or kind of the outstanding shares of Common Stock, or any other securities into which the Common Stock shall have been changed, or for which it shall have been exchanged, whether by reason of merger, consolidation or otherwise, then if the Committee, in its sole discretion, shall determine that such change equitably requires an adjustment to shares or other securities currently subject to options or Stock Units (as referred to in Section 6(d) hereof) or which may become subject to options under the Plan, or to prices or terms of outstanding options, such adjustment shall be made in accordance with such determination. In addition, in the event of such change described in this paragraph, the Committee may accelerate the time or times at which any option may be exercised or any Stock Unit may be settled and may provide for cancellation of any such accelerated option which is not exercised within a time prescribed by the Committee in its sole discretion.

(c) No right to purchase fractional shares or fractions of other securities shall result from any adjustment in options pursuant to this Section. In case of any such adjustment, the shares or other securities subject to the option shall be rounded down to the nearest whole share of Common Stock or equivalent other security, as the case may be.

9. REGISTRATION, LISTING OR QUALIFICATION OF SECURITIES

In the event that the Committee determines in its discretion that the registration, listing or qualification of the shares of Common Stock issuable under the Plan on any securities exchange or under any applicable law or governmental regulation is necessary as a condition to the issuance of such shares under the option, the option may not be exercisable or exercised in whole or in part unless such registration, listing, qualification, consent or approval has been unconditionally obtained.

10. TAX WITHHOLDING

To the extent required by applicable federal, state, local or foreign law, a Participant or optionholder shall make arrangements satisfactory to the Committee for the satisfaction of any withholding tax obligations that arise by reason of an option exercise or disposition of shares of Common Stock issued upon exercise of an option. The Corporation shall not be required to issue shares of Common Stock or to recognize the disposition of such shares until such obligations are satisfied. The Committee may permit these obligations to be satisfied by any means permitted under Section 6(a) for the payment of the exercise price of an option.

11. OPTION GRANTS BY SUBSIDIARIES

In the case of a grant of an option to any Participant employed by a Subsidiary, such grant may, if the Committee so directs, be implemented by Intel issuing any subject shares to the Subsidiary, for such lawful consideration as the Committee may determine, upon the condition or understanding that the Subsidiary will transfer the shares to the optionholder in accordance with the terms of the option specified by the Committee pursuant to the provisions of the Plan. Notwithstanding any other provision hereof, such option may be issued by and in the name of the Subsidiary and shall be deemed granted on such date as the Committee shall determine.

12. EFFECTIVE DATE, AMENDMENT AND TERMINATION OF PLAN

The Plan was adopted by Intel's Board of Directors and became effective on January 15, 1997. The Plan was amended and restated by the Board of Directors on July 16, 1997, to provide for limited transferability of options.. Unless earlier suspended or terminated by the Board of Directors, or extended as provided below, no options may be granted after the tenth anniversary of the date the Plan is approved by the Board of Directors. The Board of Directors or the Committee may from time to time extend the effective term of the Plan and otherwise amend the Plan as determined appropriate, without action by Intel's stockholders except to the extent required by applicable law. References in the Plan and in writings evidencing and setting the terms of option grants which refer to the Code or other applicable law shall also be deemed to refer to any applicable successor provisions thereof unless otherwise determined by the Committee. The Plan may be earlier terminated at such earlier time as the Board of Directors may determine. Termination and expiration of the Plan will not affect the rights and obligations arising under options theretofore granted and then in effect.

INTEL CORPORATION 1997 STOCK OPTION PLAN

ADDITIONAL INFORMATION FOR AUSTRALIAN PARTICIPANTS

This discussion has been prepared by Intel Corporation's ("Intel") solicitors to enable employees who have not previously owned stock (sometimes also referred to as shares) in an offshore company to be provided with basic information in relation to the ownership and trading of Intel stock.

This discussion is relevant for employees participating in the 1997 Plan, who are Australian residents for tax purposes, or, though not resident in Australia for tax purposes, are eligible to participate in the Plan in relation to their employment in Australia.

THE OPTIONS

- The options are to acquire Intel Corporation common stock ("Stock") in the future. Stock are commonly termed shares in Australia. The options are exercisable pursuant to the conditions set out in the Grant Agreement, which is offered under the Plan Rules.

- The exercise price of each option, which is for one unit of stock, is US$76.00. You will need to pay this sum, in US dollars, on exercise. On [date], the exercise price was equivalent to A$[________]. Exchange rates are likely to fluctuate between now and your exercise of the option.

- You may contact David Bolt at Intel Australia Pty. Ltd. on (02) 9935-5800 to obtain details of the applicable Australian Dollar equivalent of the exercise price. Conversion rates are also shown daily in most newspapers.

- The Stock issued on exercise of the options will be quoted on NASDAQ. A brief description of the NASDAQ National Market is given below. The Stock will not be quoted on the Australian Stock Exchange. To deal in the Stock, you will probably need to contact US stockbrokers.

- You will receive a copy of Intel's annual report each year which describes Intel's business.

- There are risks associated with purchasing stock in a company which you should consider before exercising your option. Owning stock does involve risk. There is no guarantee that a company's share price will rise, or that it will pay dividends or issue new stock. Share prices can fall.

- There are company specific risk factors which are described in the 10-K Statement.

NASDAQ

The stock issued to participants in the Plan on exercise of the options will be quoted on the NASDAQ National market. NASDAQ stands for National Association of Securities Dealers Automated Quotations. It is an over-the-counter trading system for securities, which has a similar purpose to a stock exchange such as the Australian Stock Exchange. It operates through a computer and telephone communications network. NASDAQ is an inter-dealer system sponsored by the National Association of Securities Dealers and is the principal over-the-counter trading system in the US. It is a computerized quotation and trading system consisting of thousands of computer terminals.

A listing with NASDAQ is voluntary. NASDAQ requires that listed companies meet certain financial standards in terms of assets and shareholder's equity. Generally these requirements are somewhat lower than those of the New York Stock Exchange and the American Stock Exchange, the two national securities exchanges operating in the US.

TAXATION IMPLICATIONS OF THE AUSTRALIAN OFFER

This discussion is relevant for Participants who are residents of Australia for tax purposes, and those who though not Australian residents, are entitled to participate in the Plan as a result of services performed in Australia. It assumes that no Australian Participant will hold more than five percent (5%) of Intel Common Stock, including Options, nor will control more than five percent (5%) of the votes which may be cast at a general meeting of Intel Corporation.

The following are the taxable events associated with the grant of Options and subsequent Stock dealings:

Grant of Options

The Options granted to you will be "qualifying rights" for Australian tax purposes and will not trigger a tax liability unless you elect to be taxed at grant.

If you elect to be taxed at grant then, you will be taxed on the deemed value of the Options in the year of grant. The "value" of the Options is determined by reference to rules in the legislation. It is a function of the market value of the Common Stock, the Option exercise price and the exercise period. By way of example, an Option to acquire stock at a price equal to the "market value" of that stock on the day of grant of the Option, and which may be exercised within ten (10) years from the date of grant, will have a deemed market value on the date of grant of 18.4% of the exercise price.

If you make this election, then you will have no further tax liability until the Stock obtained on exercise of the Option is sold, or until dividends or bonus stock are received.

It is recommended that you obtain professional tax advice before you elect to be taxed on the value of the Options at the date of grant. Ordinarily it would not be in your interest to elect to be taxed on the grant.

Exercise of Options

If you do not make the election to be taxed at the time of grant of the Options, you will be taxed on the Options in the year in which they are exercised, subject to the rules below regarding leaving employment.

If you exercise the Options and continue to hold the Stock for thirty (30) days after exercise, then the amount brought to tax will be the deemed "market value" of the Stock acquired as at the date of exercise, less the exercise price. The tax legislation sets out the formula for calculating this value.

The calculation of the amount brought to tax if the shares are sold on, or within thirty (30) days of the Options being exercised, is dealt with below.

In any event, you will need to include an amount in your tax return in the year in which the Option is exercised.

Subsequent Sale

If you sell the Stock received from the exercise of the Options on, or within thirty (30) days of, the date of the exercise of the Options, you will be subject to tax in the year in which the Options were exercised, on the consideration received for the sale of the Stock less the Option exercise price.

If the Stock received from the exercise of the Options is sold outside the thirty (30) day period from exercise, you also need to pay capital gains tax in the year of sale. A taxable capital gain will arise in the year of sale if, and to the extent that, the sale price of the Stock exceeds the deemed "market value" of the Options at the date of exercise (the value on which tax was paid on exercise of the relevant Options) plus the exercise price. This will ordinarily be the market value of the stock at the exercise date. If the Stock is sold twelve (12) months or more from the date of exercise of the Options, the taxable capital gain will be adjusted to allow for inflation.

If you made the election to be taxed on the Options in the year of the grant, the taxable capital gain which will need to be included in your taxable income on the sale of the Stock will be calculated on the basis of the sale price of the Stock less the value of the Options at the date of grant (i.e., the sum which was taxed in the year of grant) and the Option exercise price. The taxable capital gain will be adjusted to allow for inflation if the sale occurs twelve (12) months or more from the date of grant of the Options.

Leaving Employment

You will have no tax liability in respect of those Options which are forfeited on termination of employment. Further, any tax which you elected to pay on the grant of forfeited options may be refunded.

However, if you are still able to exercise the Options following termination and you had not elected to be taxed on the grant of the Options, you will be subject to tax in the year in which your employment terminates on the deemed "market value" of the Options at the date of termination of employment. You will then suffer no more tax in relation to the Options or the Stock acquired on exercise until the Stock is sold (as described above), or dividends or bonus Stock is received.

If, however, the Options are exercised and the Stock is sold within thirty (30) days of termination of your employment, you will simply be taxed on the sale price less the Option (exercise) price, and will suffer no further tax in relation to the sale of the Stock under the capital gains tax regime.

Dividends

Generally, you will be subject to tax on dividends received in Australia. The taxable sum will include the amount of US dividend withholding tax, deducted in the US before remission to you.

An Australian tax credit will be available for the US dividend withholding tax. The credit will be limited to the lesser of the amount of US withholding tax and the Australian tax applicable to the relevant amount.

The Australian and Foreign Investment Regime

The Australian foreign Investment Fund (FIF) regime operates to tax Australian residents holding interests in certain foreign companies on the increase of value of that interest each year, whether or not realized.

The Common Stock of Intel Corporation is presently listed on NASDAQ and the FIF regime will not apply to your Intel Corporation holding. Intel Corporation will advise you if this position changes.

Withholding and Reporting

Intel Corporation has no obligation to report the grant or exercise of your Options or stock to the Australian tax authorities or to withhold the proceeds of any exercise. Accordingly, you will be solely responsible for reporting your gains to the Australian Taxation Office and paying any required taxes.

Summary

This summary only briefly discusses the Australian tax consequences of benefits acquired under the Plan, based on law currently in effect.

Due to the complexities of, and possible changes to, the tax law you should seek professional tax advice.

CASE STUDIES & WORKSHEETS

II. Worksheets

If you have stock options that have been granted by your employer, it's important that you know what you have, the percentage of your overall compensation these options make up, and how much your options are potentially worth.

On the following two pages are worksheets you can use to keep track of your options; refer to them as you and your financial advisor go over your finances. Remember: you'll want to update the information regularly as your situation changes.

CASE STUDIES & WORKSHEETS

Figuring Value

What type of stock options do I have? ______________________

How many stock options do I have? ______________________

What is the strike price for these options? ______________________

What is the current market value of these options?

____

____

How much could I potentially gain when I exercise the options (current market value minus the strike price)?

____

____

____

Are any of my options currently underwater (meaning their market value is less than the strike price)? How many? What percentage of my portfolio do they make up? And do I think it's likely that the market value of the stock will go up before my options expire?

____

____

____

____

____

____

CASE STUDIES & WORKSHEETS

Vesting Schedule

Many employers grant their employees a number of options, and these options vest according to a schedule of one to five years or more. An option is considered "vested" when you can use it to purchase stock, and typically the vesting schedule will be laid out in your option agreement. Use this worksheet to keep track of which options are vesting when.

Grant Date	Vesting Date	Percentage of Portfolio

Core Area 7

Resources for Further Research

I. Recommended Books

Pastore, Robert R. Stock Options: *An Authoritative Guide to Incentive and Nonqualified Stock Options*. 2nd Edition. PCM Capital Publishing, 2000.
This is a thorough resource book on employee stock options.

Thomas, Kaye A. *Consider Your Options*. Lisle, Illinois: Fairmark Press, Inc., 2000.
This is a detailed introduction to the ins and outs of employee stock options and employee stock purchase plans, written by a leading tax lawyer and author.

Thomsett, Michael. *Getting Started in Options*. 3rd Edition. John Wiley & Sons, 1997.
This is a good book for beginners who want to learn about investing in stock options; it is particularly useful for its discussion of option strategy.

II. Recommended Websites

The Chicago Board Options Exchange
www.cboe.com
This is the site of the Chicago Board Options Exchange (CBOE), and it's a great place to get information about options trading.

The Internal Revenue Service
www.irs.gov
If you want to learn more about taxes and stock options, why not go directly to the source? Through the IRS website, you can get just about any form or booklet that you need, and the helpful search feature lets you home in exactly where you need to go.

The National Center for Employee Ownership
www.nceo.org
The National Center for Employee Ownership provides a lot of helpful information and statistics about a variety of employee ownership programs, including stock options.

Schaeffer's Investment Research
www.schaeffersresearch.com
The website of Schaeffer's Investment Research is a good place for beginners to get their feet wet in the world of options trading.

Tax Guide for Investors
www.fairmark.com
This is a website created and maintained by Kay A. Thomas, a tax lawyer and author of *Consider Your Options*. It provides information about taxes, investing and other topics.

III. Bibliography

"A Brief History of Stock Options." Schaeffer's Investment Research. www.schaeffersresearch.com/option/basics/history.htm

Anderson, Ralph, CPA. "The Tax Expert: Options, Settlements, Trusts." CNBC.com. www.cnbc.com/commentary/commentary_full_story_tax_center.asp?storyid=22037

Bittman, James. *Options for the Stock Investor*. Burr Ridge, Illinois: Irwin Professional Publishing, 1995.

Buckman, Rebecca. "Microsoft Offers Perks to Retain Top Talent." Careerjournal.com. October 27, 2000.

"Differentiating Between In-, At-, and Out-of-the-Money Stock Options." Shaeffer's Investment Research. www.schaeffersresearch.com/option/basics/in_out.htm

Fairclough, Gordon. "Philip Morris to Pay Special Bonuses To Executives, Citing 'Unusual Year." Careerjournal.com. October 27, 2000.

"Frequently Asked Questions." Chicago Board Options Exchange. www.cboe.com/education/faq.htm

Harroch, Richard D. *Business Contracts Kit for Dummies*. Foster City, CA: IDG Books Worldwide, Inc., 2000.

RESOURCES FOR FURTHER RESEARCH

"How Stocks and Stock Options Differ." Schaeffer's Investment Research. www.schaeffersresearch.com/option/basics/differ.htm

"Incentive Stock Options vs. Nonstatutory Stock Options." CNBC.com. www.cnbc.com/commentary/commentary_full_story_sbc.asp?storyid=21361

McCormally, Kevin. "Taxing Exercise." Kiplinger.com. May, 2000. www.kiplinger.com/magazine/archives/2000/May/managing/qa-manage2.htm

Mollison, Caitlin. "The Ins and Outs of Stock Options." CNBC.com. www.cnbc.com/commentary/commentary_full_story_wic.asp?storyid=21836

Pastore, Robert R. *Stock Options: An Authoritative Guide to Incentive and Nonqualified Stock Options*. 2nd Edition. PCM Capital Publishing, 2000.

Roemer, John. "The Dark Side of Employee Stock Options." TheStandard.com. December 12, 2000.

"Stock Options Aren't Just for Big Shots Anymore." *Kiplinger's Magazine*. April 1999. www.kiplinger.com/magazine/archives/1999/April

Taxable and Non Taxable Income. IRS Publication 525.

RESOURCES FOR FURTHER RESEARCH

"Taxes and Investing: A Guide for the Individual Investor." Chicago Board of Options Exchange. www.cboe.com/resources/tax.htm

"The Basics." Chicago Board Options Exchange. www.cboe.com/education/

Thomas, Kaye. A. *Consider Your Options*. Lisle, Illinois: Fairmark Press, Inc., 2000.

Thomsett, Michael C. *Getting Started in Options*. 3rd Edition. John Wiley & Sons, 2000.

"Two Types of Stock Option Contracts." Schaeffer's Investment Research. www.schaeffersresearch.com/option/basics/call&put.htm

Yang, Lena Lee. "Employee Stock Options." FinancialFinesse.com. www.financialfinesse.com/index.cgi?display_297=1

--. "Employee Stock Options: Tax Tips." FinancialFinesse.com. www.financialfinesse.com/index.cgi?display_352=1

--. "Exercising Your Options." FinancialFinesse.com. www.financialfinesse.com/index.cgi?display_334=1

Core Area 8

Key Words Glossary

Alternative Minimum Tax (AMT)
The Alternative Minimum Tax (AMT) is a federal tax that you may owe when you exercise an incentive stock option (ISO) or have long-term capital gains.

Basis
For the purposes of figuring capital gains taxes, your basis is, essentially, where you start with a stock or other investment; your basis is used to figure taxes and profits.

Call
In options trading, a call gives you the right, but not the obligation, to sell a stock at a specified price.

Capital Gain/Capital Loss
Capital gains are the income that you earn when you sell a capital asset – which can be anything other than products that you sell as part of a business – that has appreciated in value. A capital loss comes when you sell a capital asset that has depreciated in value; in other words, you sell it for less than the amount for which you purchased it.

Compensation Income
Compensation income is considered “ordinary income,” i.e., money that you earn for being employed by a company. You can earn compensation income either as a regular employee or an

independent contractor, and when you exercise nonqualified stock options (NQSOs) you will need to report the difference between the exercise price and the fair market value of the stock as compensation income.

Exercise
When you purchase stock from an option grant, it is called "exercising" the options. You will exercise your options at a pre-determined price, called the "strike price," which will have been spelled out in your option agreement.

Fair Market Value
Fair market value is the price of a stock on the stock exchange at a given time on a given day. If the stock is not publicly traded, fair market value is determined by other methods, including internal evaluation methods of a company or the evaluation from a third party evaluator.

Holding Period
If you exercise incentive stock options (ISOs), you will receive favorable tax treatment on the exercise if you hold the options for one year from the date of exercise or two years from the date of the granting of the options – whichever is greater. Note that this means a year (or two) plus at least one day. This time period is called the holding period. If you exercise the options before the holding period is up, it is called an "early disposition."

In the Money/Out of the Money
For traditional employer granted options – nonqualified or incentive stock options – your stock options are considered in the money if the underlying stock is worth more than the exercise price. They are called out of the money (or "underwater") if the stock is worth

less than the exercise price. In options trading, with call options and put options, what is at the money, in the money and out of the money differs slightly. Both put and call options are considered to be at the money if the exercise price is equal to the current price of the stock. Put and call options are reversed, however, in what is considered in or out of the money. A put option is out of the money when its strike price is less than the current price of the underlying stock, and in the money when its strike price is greater than the current price of the stock. Conversely, a call option is out of the money when the strike price is greater than the stock's market price, and in the money when the strike price is less than the stock's current price.

LEAPS
Long-term Equity Anticipation Securities – or LEAPS – are relatively long-term options contracts that you can buy. They typically expire three years from the date the contract is first listed.

Premium
The price of an option on the options market is known as its premium.

Put
In options trading, a put gives you the right, but not the obligation, to sell a stock at a specified price.

Reload Options
Also sometimes known as restoration or replacement options, reload options are employer-granted options that you can receive by turning in shares of stock that you already own. This method of obtaining options is only available if your company specifies that it allows for it. Reload options are beneficial in that they let you cash

in on the money for your options when they are in the money, and lock in new options that allow for the potential of even greater profits.

Spread
The spread is the difference between an option's exercise price and the fair market value of the stock. Spread is used to figure income, basis, and other key numbers on your exercise. It may also affect when you decide to exercise your options, since you might want to wait until there is a large spread between the exercise price and the value of the stock.

Strike Price
The strike price is the price at which your options are fixed; it is also the price at which you can exercise the options, or the exercise price.

Vested
Your options are vested, essentially, when you are allowed to exercise them. Your company may establish a "vesting schedule," which grants you options at a particular strike price, but then has a timetable according to which you can exercise them. The underlying stock upon which options are based can also be vested – meaning that there may be a timetable according to which you can or cannot sell this stock, even after you have exercised your options.

Become a Part of OneHourWiz™

- Publish a Quick Tip on an Upcoming Topic (50-5,000 words)
- Submit an Idea to Write an Entire OneHourWiz
- Post Comments on the Topics Mentioned
- Read Expanded Excerpts
- Free Excerpts From Upcoming Guides
- Links for More Information on a Topic

www.OneHourWiz.com

Order These Other Great OneHourWiz™ Guides Today!

OneHourWiz: Making Your First Million

By Jon Pirone, ISBN: 1587621037

OneHourWiz: Making Your First Million presents ways for every individual to make their first million. Three main focal areas are covered including investing, starting your own business, and taking equity as a form of compensation. The guide is a very practical and entertaining look at ways for anyone to make their first million. The guide also includes interviews with some of the most successful business people of our time who explain how they "made their first million."

OneHourWiz: Becoming a Techie

By Mary Pyefinch, ISBN: 1587621045

OneHourWiz: Becoming a Techie is a whirlwind tour of computer technology presented in an easy to understand language and format that both technology novices and experts will find useful and entertaining. Readers will learn about computers, networks, programming, the Internet, telecommunications and wireless. After reading this guide, any individual will have the knowledge and guidance to "talk the talk" of the techies. The guide also includes interviews with leading CTOs from companies such as Motley Fool, Symantec, Verisign, Flooz.com and others who help break down the language of the techies!

OneHourWiz: Personal PR & Making a Name For Yourself

By Colleen Inches, ISBN: 1587621061

Have you ever wished you could sell yourself the way advertisers promote products? Wouldn't you love to say, "Hey world, here I am. I'm the best product in the market!" It's no coincidence the most successful people in business do it everyday, and so can you. Colleen Burns Inches shows you how to use self promotion in any career or aspect of your life. Inches, a former television news producer in New York City, gives you step by step instructions on getting attention, recognition and even media coverage for your ideas and events.

OneHourWiz: Internet Freelancing (Easy to Implement Ways to Making a Little or a Lot of Extra Money on the Internet)

By Rachel Vine, ISBN: 1587620030

OneHourWiz: Internet Freelancing contains the most up to date information on how to use the Internet to make a little, or a lot, of extra money on the Internet. The guide covers every opportunity available on the Internet including getting Paid-to-Surf the web, test new Internet products and services, freelance writing, part time consulting opportunities, affiliate programs, or simply getting paid on a monthly basis by having an extra task bar on your browser. Whether you are looking to make an extra $25 a month or an extra $2,500 a month, this guide will pay for itself many times over within the first month alone.

OneHourWiz: Internet and Technology Careers (After the Shakedown)

By April Griffin, ISBN: 1587620049

Want to take advantage of the perks Internet and technology companies have to offer? This guide will help make sure you know what to look for, ask the right questions, and get the right things put into writing so you have your upside (such as options and bonuses) and downside (guaranteed employment clauses) covered. You've heard the hype. Now learn how to use all the buzzwords with authority. Discover the workplace trends - where the hot jobs can be found, the training you need, and the salary to expect. Read interviews with recruiters from international job placement firm Kforce.com as well as computerjobs.com. Regardless of whether you are already in the Internet and technology industry or are looking to break through, this is the guide for you!

OneHourWiz: Stock Options

By Vivian Wagner, ISBN: 1587621053

Stock options are being granted to record numbers of employees, but many people receiving stock options don't really understand what they are. This guide gives you the information you need to make informed decisions about stock options, including how to value them and your company, the difference between Incentive Stock Options (ISOs) and Nonqualified Stock Options (NQSOs), the tax consequences of exercising your options, as well as information for those who want to get into options trading on their own-in an easy to understand language and format. This OneHourWiz guide also includes interviews with noted experts in the field, lawyers from some of the top law firms in the world, CFOs from companies such as Hoovers, LifeMinders,

Register.com, a sample stock option plan from Intel, and worksheets to help you keep track of your stock options.

OneHourWiz: Landing Your First Job

By Andrew Goldsmith, ISBN: 1587620253

Are you a college senior terrified to graduate? Or a freshman with a lot of foresight? This is the guide you need to make sure your first step into the real world takes you in the right direction (and to start thinking ahead to that second step!). You'll get advice from the director of Career Services at one of the hottest Ivy League schools in the country and advice from such experts as the head of recruiting from PriceWaterhouseCoopers. You'll read the stories of people who just a few years ago were standing exactly where you are, and are now establishing themselves at dotcoms, consulting firms, finance jobs, and even in the publishing, entertainment and theater scenes!

OneHourWiz: Public Speaking

By Sporty King, ISBN: 1587621096

OneHourWiz: Public Speaking can help anyone master the art of public speaking. Whether giving a presentation to a few individuals, presenting to thousands of people, or just wanting to speak more confidently to others, this guide will give you all of the keys to success as a public speaker in an easy to understand format and language. This proprietary process used to become a public speaker employed by Sporty King, a renowned public speaker, is sure to get you speaking confidently in no time.

New Titles Available Every Month!

Visit Your Local Bookseller Today!

Visit www.OneHourWiz.com for a Complete List of Titles

About the Author

Vivian A. Wagner, Ph.D.

Vivian A. Wagner, Ph.D. is a freelance writer specializing in personal finance, business, technology, health, and creative nonfiction. Her articles have appeared in a variety of print and Web-based publications, including *American Profile, Bank Systems & Technology*, *E-Cruiting Today*, FinancialFinesse.com, *The Herb Quarterly,* and *The Plain Dealer.* She has published one previous book – *Aging and Elder Care* (2000, Parlay International). Wagner has a Ph.D. in English from the University of Illinois, Urbana-Champaign, and she lives with her husband and two children in New Concord, Ohio.

ACKNOWLEDGMENTS

Thanks to my mother, who gave me a head for numbers. My early tutelage under her created the foundation for my work as a personal finance journalist. Thanks, too, must go to my husband, Dr. Todd Lekan, who despite a busy teaching schedule somehow finds time both to listen to my ideas and to help manage the household while I do my writing. Thanks to Jason Edwards and everyone else at Aspatore Books for choosing me to do this project and for working with me to see it to completion. Finally, thanks to my children, for continually reminding me that there's more to life than thinking and writing about money.

OneHourWiz™

The Legendary, World-Famous Method to Mastering Anything in an Hour

How do I become a OneHourWiz?

OneHourWiz is a proven, unique method of learning that focuses on the fundamental principles of a topic, along with advice from industry experts, to master the most important aspects of anything in an hour. Although not always known by the name OneHourWiz, the principles behind this important method of learning have been practiced for decades by leading executives of the world's largest companies, top government officials, federal intelligence agencies, and some of the world's most renowned professors, teachers and visionaries.

Most people do not realize that when trying to learn a new subject or topic, they spend 80% of their time not focusing on the right principles. If they were to receive instruction from the right teachers, focused on the right principles, they could learn anything in a fraction of the time. However, getting all of these industry leaders, teachers and visionaries together would be virtually impossible. Therefore, our OneHourWiz authors collect the most important pieces of information from these individuals, pour through volumes of research, talk with industry leaders and present the material in a condensed and easy to understand format.

So, how is it possible to master anything in an hour? Each OneHourWiz uses a proprietary method that focuses on 8 core areas including: The 10 Most Important Principles, The History/Background Information, Focal Points/Technique, Interviews With Industry Visionaries, Quick Tips, Case Studies & Worksheets, Resources for Further Research, and a Key Words Glossary so you can "talk the talk." OneHourWiz guides have become overnight classics that remain with our readers for years and years as timeless guides they can always refer back to. So sit back, relax, and enjoy the following pages on your way to becoming a OneHourWiz!